Science 6

for Christian Schools®

"Thus saith the Lord the maker thereof, the Lord that formed it, to establish it; the Lord is his name; Call unto me, and I will answer thee, and shew thee great and mighty things, which thou knowest not."
Jeremiah 33:2-3

Dawn L. Watkins

NOTE:

The fact that materials produced by other publishers are referred to in this volume does not constitute an endorsement by Bob Jones University Press of the content or theological position of materials produced by such publishers. The position of the Bob Jones University Press, and the University itself, is well known. Any references and ancillary materials are listed as an aid to the student or the teacher and in an attempt to maintain the accepted academic standards of the publishing industry.

SCIENCE 6 for Christian Schools®
Second Edition

Dawn L. Watkins

Produced in cooperation with the Bob Jones University Department of Science Education of the School of Education, the College of Arts and Science, and Bob Jones Elementary School.

for Christian Schools is a registered trademark of Bob Jones University Press.

ISBN 0-89084-437-2   (hardbound)
ISBN 0-89084-624-3   (softbound)

15   14   13   12   11   10   9   8   7

Contents

 # Earthquakes

"And there was trembling in the host, in the field, and among all the people: the garrison, and the spoilers, they also trembled, and the earth quaked: so it was a very great trembling."

I Samuel 14:15

The afternoon seemed no different from any other. People were leaving work, shopping in the malls, waiting for the World Series game to begin. Then there was a rumble, like thunder underground, a deep roar beneath the highways, the stores, the playing fields. Dogs barked, and people hesitated in their tracks, listening.

The rumble became a violent shaking. People ran for the open ball field, for doorways, for parking lots. Shelves toppled over, walls caved in, lawns split open, roads buckled, bridges fell, and still the earth shook. It lurched then, like some giant door giving way. Cars plunged into gaps that broke open in the highways, and whole buildings dropped into piles of rubble. Bricks and flying glass spewed from houses. People died in their cars as tons of concrete from overpasses smashed down.

In fifteen seconds, the earth was still again. The people who were not hurt stood dazed and silent. Dust filtered up from the new ruins. Fires burst out from broken gas lines. And then began the long ordeal of finding the dead and the injured, of putting the city back together again.

In less time than it took you to read those first paragraphs, the city of San Francisco, on October 17, 1989, suffered millions of dollars of damage and lost more than one hundred of its citizens. This was a major earthquake, and not the first to hit that city. What causes such massive wrenchings in the earth is still mostly a mystery.

Theories on Causes of Earthquakes

Hundreds of years ago, people explained earthquakes with marvelous stories. The Japanese believed that the earth sat on the back of a monster spider. When the spider jumped, the earth shook. Other ancient people thought that the gods were fighting, rocking the earth as they struck one another.

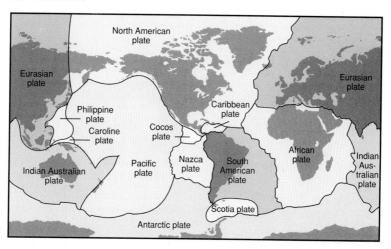

Modern theories about earthquakes are just as amazing in their own way. Many scientists believe that the surface of the earth, the crust, is a patchwork of moving pieces called *plates*. You might think of the crust as a jigsaw puzzle floating on hot wax. The wax is like the earth's mantle. The mantle always seems to be moving, causing the plates to move. You cannot usually feel the plates moving because they move so slowly–hardly as fast as your fingernails grow.

The lines along which the puzzle pieces touch are called *faults*. When the puzzle pieces shift, they can slide alongside each other. If the pieces snag against each other, preventing their movement, pressure builds up along the edges of the pieces. Imagine that the puzzle has little houses and trees atop it. What would happen when one puzzle piece suddenly slipped? The top, or crust, would become uneven, disrupting everything above it. There would be an "earthquake." Real earthquakes happen much the same way as the puzzle was jolted—only on a gigantic scale.

If you bend a stick slowly until it almost breaks, you build up in the stick a great deal of tension. The tendency of the molecules in the stick to stay together is pitted against the force you impose by bending the stick. The tension must be relieved eventually. Either the stick will snap, or you will quit bending it. Earthquakes may result from similar events.

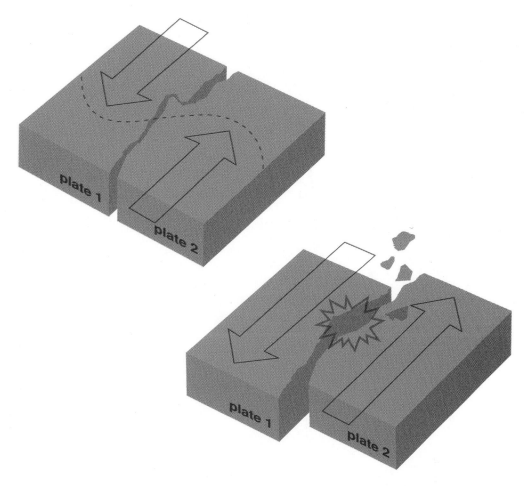

The plates of the crust push and scrape against each other, building up tension until something gives. One of the plates may shift abruptly along the other, releasing tremendous amounts of stored-up energy. If the tension is released all at once, rocks break apart and whole sections of the earth's crust are jerked out of their positions. Everything above the ground is affected dramatically–the more energy released, the greater the drama. Sometimes the shaking is so small that no one feels it. Only the sensitive instruments of scientists recording earthquakes show that anything happened. Other times the quake feels like a hundred large tractor-trailers roaring by. And once in a while, the ground shudders so that cities fall to ruin and thousands of people die in seconds.

Finding Out . . .

About Earthquakes

1. Get a balance scale, modeling clay, two letter-size envelope boxes, some sand, some water, several toothpicks, a quart jar, and a small sprinkling can or plant sprayer.

2. You may want to cut the boxes down an inch or so in height. Cut a small V-notch in one end of each box. With the modeling clay, build a mountain in one envelope box (keep the higher slope on the unnotched side) and an ocean basin in the other. Be sure to pull the clay up the sides of the ocean box, to prevent leaking.

3. Put one box on each side of the balance scale, the notched sides together. Put some water in the ocean basin. Add enough sand to the mountain box to balance the sides. Make sure that the boxes touch squarely. Make a thin seal with modeling clay over the surface where the two boxes touch. Lay some toothpicks straight across the line on either side of the notch.

4. Make a small vent at the end of the "ocean" for overflow water. Holding the jar under the vent, sprinkle some water on the sand until the water and sand run into the ocean. What happens when the sides become unbalanced? What happens to the toothpicks? Theorize how some earthquakes may be caused.

Pressures that create earthquakes may be caused by changes on the surface of or under the crust. When erosion, for example, adds weight or removes weight from an area, the imbalance may create tension on a fault. Over a few years, the tension builds to the breaking point. Man has even caused a few minor earthquakes by testing nuclear bombs underground.

Scientists think that many events are occurring all the time under the earth's crust. Scientists who hold this view think that under ''hot spots''—places where there is a lot of earthquake and volcanic activity—are areas of boiling rock deep in the mantle. Hot, roiling rock 1,800 miles (2,896.2 km) below the surface, for example, may be causing a vast swelling on the floor of the Pacific Ocean. The bulge is 2,000 miles (3,218 km) wide; it has changed the sea level. How do you think the changes in the sea might affect the tension on the plates of the crust?

Recording Earthquakes

People who go through an earthquake have different ways of describing what happened. Some say that there was a roar; some say there was not. Some say the shaking was severe; some say it was not. Some say that the quake went on for five minutes; some say it lasted for only a few seconds. How people remember the experience depends on where they were, if they were awake or asleep when it started, how observant they are, how excitable they are, and many other things.

Even if a clear-headed, well-trained earthquake expert were there, his observations would be limited by his senses (he cannot see and hear and feel everything) and by his experience (a man who had been in an earthquake before might view the present quake differently from a man who had only read about such things). Scientists need more objective ways of describing quakes.

The roar and tremble of an earthquake are the ways we perceive the mighty vibrations caused by the slipping

plates of the earth's crust. Particles all around the slipping point are set into violent motion, banging into each other, setting off chain reactions of movement. When this chain reaction hits the open air, we hear the vibrations as noise. If you bend a stick until it breaks, you will hear a snap, a sound resulting from molecules separating suddenly.

As you break the stick, you will also feel a stinging in your hands. Why do you think your hands sting? The vibrations from the breaking of the stick travel down to your hands and cause the cells in your hand to move. Why do you think it stings more to break a large stick than a small one? The traveling vibrations in the earth during a quake are called *seismic waves*.

The slipping point, or *focus,* for most quakes is below the surface of the ground. The seismic waves go out from the focus in all directions. Some reach the surface and continue to travel along the top; these are *L* waves. Some go toward the center of the earth; these are the *P* and the *S* waves. You might compare the light radiating from the sun with the vibrations traveling out from the focus of an earthquake. Does the sun produce light only in the plane in which the planets orbit? No, and neither does an earthquake shake only the surface of the ground.

Since the effects of an earthquake are vibrations, scientists devised an instrument to record movement in the earth. It is called a *seismograph,* from two Greek words meaning "quake" and "to write." The seismograph literally writes the vibrations on paper, allowing scientists to see how hard the earth shook.

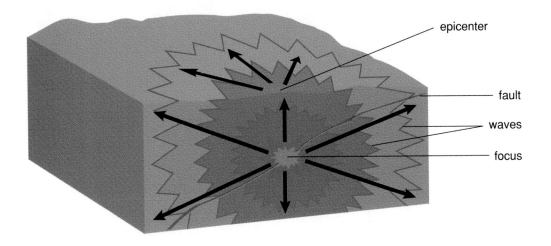

Seismographic Record:

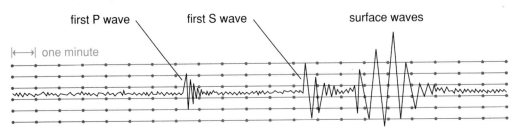

first P wave   first S wave   surface waves

|←→| one minute

Early seismographs were basically pens hanging from string over a roll of paper. When the ground shook, the paper shook–and the pen, tending to stay still, traced a line on the moving paper. More modern equipment uses lasers to trace lines on photosensitive paper. A timer marks the minutes as the paper rolls by. Why do you think it is important to have the time recorded? That way, researchers know exactly when the quake began and how long it lasted.

The best seismographs record up-and-down, north-south, and east-west movements. Why do you think it is important to record all those different movements? Earthquakes do not shake the earth in just one direction. Sometimes the seismic waves are so strong that the surface of the ground ripples like water after a rock is dropped into it. In that case, the ground moves up and down and outward all at once.

Finding Out . . .

About Seismographs

1. Get a paper-towel holder, a roll of paper towels, a felt-tip pen, modeling clay, and a large eye screw. Also get one of the following groups of items: some picture wire, a piece of plywood just slightly bigger than the towel holder, some screws for the towel holder, and a structure that will extend over the table, such as a crookneck lamp; or a wooden crate, some screws for the towel holder, and a cup hook; or materials to build a frame over the seismograph and a cup hook.

2. Secure the towel holder to the inside of the crate or to the frame you have constructed or to the plywood. Place the plywood on the table or desk.

3. Use the clay to make a ball about the size of a tennis ball. Push the top of the felt marker into the ball until the pen is steady. Directly opposite the pen, push in the eye screw. Press the clay around the pen and the screw so that they will not slip out.

4. If you are using a crate, screw the cup hook into the crate, centered over the towel rack. If you are using a frame, screw the cup hook into the underside of the top bar. Hang the eye screw from the cup hook. Place the crate or frame on the table or desk. If you are using a crookneck lamp or something similar, loop some picture wire through the eye screw and then over the neck of the lamp. Position the lamp over the towel holder so that the pen falls at the middle of the roll of towels. Adjust either the pen in the clay or the height of the table or lamp until the pen tip just touches the paper-towel roll.

5. Carefully and slowly pull the towels off the roll toward you. The pen should make a straight line in the middle of the towel. Mark one towel this way. Then as you continue to pull the towels, have a partner gently nudge the table. What happens to the line on the towels? Pull another towel through and have your partner bump the table a little harder. Compare the mark of the first ''tremor'' with the bigger quake. Can you think of a way to measure the up-and-down movement of a quake?

Interpreting Records of Earthquakes

There may be as many as one million earthquakes on earth in a year. Most are too small to cause any damage or even to be felt. Some produce only minor problems, such as rattling windows and making pictures hang crooked. Such quakes are usually called *tremors*. Only a few each year are called major earthquakes. But how do experts decide what qualifies as a major earthquake?

In 1935 the American scientist Charles Richter came up with a scale for ranking quakes. Looking at seismograph readings, Richter assigned each recorded quake a *magnitude,* a number representing how large its seismic waves were. Each whole number on the scale represents a quake that produced waves ten times larger than the number before it. That is, a quake of magnitude 7 produces waves ten times larger than a quake of magnitude 6. How would you compare a magnitude 6 with a magnitude 8? Most scientists call any quake of 7 or greater a major earthquake. Since the development of the Richter scale, the largest earthquake has been in Alaska. That 1964 quake is ranked between 8.6 and 8.9. But because it occurred in a place where few people lived, only 114 lives were lost.

The amount of energy–or *intensity*–represented on the scale increases by more than ten times for each number. A magnitude 7 releases thirty times as much energy as a magnitude 6. A quake ranked as a 2.5 on the Richter scale releases as much energy as 1,000 gallons (3,780.5 liters) of burning gasoline. A magnitude 8.5 quake releases about as much energy as 1 trillion gallons (3.8 trillion liters).

When a major earthquake occurs somewhere, seismographs in many parts of the world register the event. By comparing the readings on each quake, researchers have made some guesses about the inside of our planet. Since all waves do not travel through the earth at the same speed or in a perfect arc, scientists think the readings indicate differences in the materials of the mantle and core. Can you make any guesses about the structure of the earth by looking at the drawing?

The most recent theories about the inside of the earth compare the mantle to the atmosphere we live in. Just as warm air rises and cooler air sinks, so hot molten rock rises, cools slightly, and descends again toward the core. This internal "weather" is what keeps the mantle moving and the surface of our world in constant risk of quakes and volcanoes. The inner core of the earth seems to be solid, heavy, and dense.

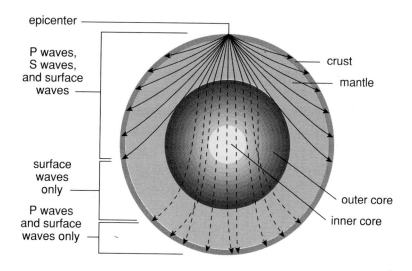

Scientists also use the many seismographic recordings to determine where the center of an earthquake was. They can find the *epicenter,* the point on the surface directly above the focus. What do you think the prefix "epi-" means? By comparing the specific times that the seismographs showed ground movement, researchers can estimate how far their stations were from the center.

If you were at a station and determined that the earthquake was 100 miles (160.9 km) away, how would you show the possible positions of the quake on a map? Will it help you to know that you need a compass to draw with? You would put the point of the compass on your station on the map, and using the scale of miles as a guide, set the pencil arm. If, for example, the scale was $\frac{1}{4}$ inch equals 50 miles, where would you set the pencil arm for 100 miles? At $\frac{1}{2}$ inch. Then you would draw a circle all around the station on the map. You would know that somewhere on that line, the quake had occurred. How will one station use the other stations' findings to pinpoint the epicenter?

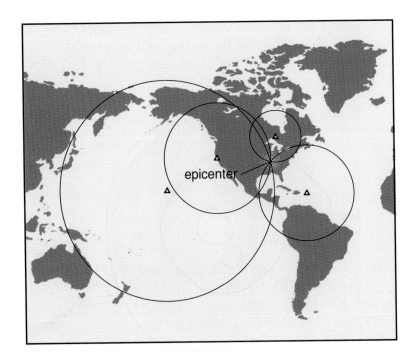

epicenter

Finding Out . . .

About Epicenters

1. Get your notebook, a compass, three colored pencils, and a ruler.

2. Follow the directions in your notebook and find the epicenters. Color each epicenter a different color.

3. Which earthquake do you think was highest on the Richter scale? Why?

ACTION

Seismology

Seismology is the study of earthquakes. Seismologists try to find out all they can every time and anywhere the earth shakes. It is their hope to be able someday to predict earthquakes just as we can now predict hurricanes. Presently, however, they do well to gather and sort the information that becomes available during the few seconds the earth's crust is shuddering somewhere.

Some seismologists set up lasers and reflectors across fault lines. They can tell whether the plates have moved by measuring how long it takes the light to travel to the reflectors and back. Others keep watch over sensors set 1,000 feet (304.8 m) underground. They hope to get a bit of advance notice that a quake is coming.

Several seismologists have moved to Parkfield, California, to study earthquakes. Since Parkfield gets an earthquake about every twenty-two years and because it sits directly over the famous San Andreas fault, scientists believe it is due for a magnitude 5 or 6 quake in the early 1990s. Parkfield is not expecting much damage: only thirty-four people live there (not counting seismologists).

In Parkfield and many other places, seismologists patiently wait for the ground to shake again. They especially want to collect information about what happens right before a quake begins. Why do you think it is not enough to document one earthquake well? Do you think that what happens in Parkfield will be true for an earthquake somewhere else—or even in Parkfield the next time?

Earthquakes in History

San Francisco was famous for earthquakes long before 1989. In 1906 the city was rocked by a huge quake. Some places in the San Andreas fault jumped apart 21 feet (6.4 m). The earth split open, like a cloth tearing, at more than 7,000 miles (11,263 km) an hour. Nearly 700 people died, and thousands lost all their property. Jack London, a writer in the city, recorded the devastation: "San Francisco is gone! Nothing remains of it but the memories. . . . All the shrewd contrivances and safeguards of man had been thrown out of gear by the 30 seconds' twitching of the earth's crust." Scientists today estimate the quake was an 8.3. How does that compare with the 1989 quake?

Before the Richter scale, people could rank a quake only by the destruction it caused. The most destructive earthquake in history hit Shensi, China, in 1556. As many as 800,000 may have died in that disaster. In 1897, a quake hit India and was felt over almost two million square miles. The studies on this earthquake marked the beginning of seismology. The 1989 quake in San Francisco measured between 6.9 and 7.1. How would you classify it? Should there be a magnitude 10 anywhere in the world, it would probably be felt everywhere.

Throughout history, people have believed that the earth can open up, swallow men and houses and even cities, and close again without a trace. When the earth shook, some feared being snatched away without a clue more than they feared dying in the rubble of a building. In the quake that hit Port Royal, Jamaica, in 1692, a merchant was walking to the docks when the earth opened under his feet and he fell into the mud below. When the tidal wave smashed inland, the crack flooded, and the merchant, still living, was swept out to sea. There a boat picked him up.

Despite such reports, scientists have not seen any evidence that the earth swallows anything during earthquakes. They have observed sand or loose earth slipping down into a crack that opens. But in all the annals of earthquake history, they say, there is no proof that the ground ever gaped wide and then snapped shut over anything, like some monstrous mouth.

Moses and Aaron and the children of Israel, however, saw such a thing happen to Korah and his followers. Numbers 16 tells how the Lord made "a new thing," and "the earth opened her mouth, and swallowed them up, and their houses, and all the men that appertained unto Korah, and all their goods. They, and all that appertained to them, went down alive into the pit, and the earth closed upon them: and they perished from among the congregation."

The Alaska quake caused another phenomenon called a *tsunami,* a massive tidal wave. Tsunamis happen when quakes suddenly change the lay of the ocean floor or when landslides plunge into the seas from shaken landmasses. These waves can travel as fast as 500 miles (800 km) an hour. One tsunami on the coast of Siberia broke at over 210 feet (64 m) high. When such waves crash onto a shore, they are often more deadly than the earthquakes that caused them.

By studying earthquake records, both ancient and modern, scientists have observed that almost 80 per cent of quakes happen along a band around the Pacific Ocean called *the ring of fire.* This band stretches along western South America, up the California coast, across the Pacific Ocean, along the Asian coast, and down to Australia. Another band, the *Mediterranean belt,* produces about 15 per cent of earthquakes. Not all quakes occur where plates meet; some happen in the middle of plates, like the Missouri quakes of 1811 and 1812, which may have been close to magnitude 8. Scientists know even less about such earthquakes than they do about those that occur on faults.

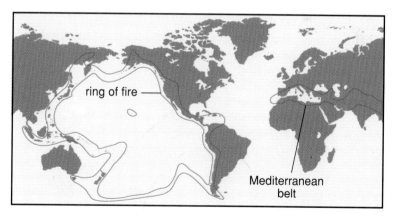

The only prediction that scientists can really make is to say that places that have had earthquakes before will probably have them again. Any cities on or near faults are at more risk than other cities. But an earthquake can strike anywhere at any time. Look at the map above. What areas can be most sure of future earthquakes?

When you view the ground we walk on as part of a continent that is riding along on a giant plate, a plate which itself is floating, the phrase "solid earth" means little. The new ideas about how the earth is made up have caused many people to live in uncertainty and dread. They feel helpless against the great, unpredictable powers of the planet.

Others, like many who live around the San Andreas fault, adopt a casual attitude, deciding not to worry too much about what they cannot control or even to think about earthquakes at all. Still other people pack up and move somewhere else, hoping to find a place not troubled by such natural disasters.

The Christian can look on the discoveries and theories about the earth with wonder rather than with fear because he knows God is in charge of all that happens. The drifting and colliding plates do not make him feel insignificant or unprotected. He can see earthquakes as forces God established to build up mountains, to change oceans and rivers, to help keep the earth renewing itself. He can take comfort even in disaster, believing that He who created the earth knows best how to rule it. The Christian can feel the earth shake beneath his feet and trust his God to care for him and to bring all things to pass according to His plan.

"And there were voices, and thunders, and lightnings; and there was a great earthquake, such as was not since men were upon the earth, so mighty an earthquake, and so great."

Revelation 16:18

 # Volcanoes

"And the mountains shall be molten under him, and the valleys shall be cleft, as wax before the fire, and as the waters that are poured down a steep place."

Micah 1:4

The day was sweltering hot in the Roman city. The bakers and the pressers of togas complained to each other about their work. In a public square, a servant collected water from the carved fountain; in a villa nearby, a noble-woman poured wine from a silver pitcher. An artist put the last details on the family portrait he had been hired to paint on the walls of a rich house. Traders who had recently arrived in port sat in an inn eating bread and fruit. In an alley, a teen-ager scrawled the name of his girlfriend on a doorpost. In a huge theater, actors rehearsed for a play. Outside, children ran along the raised sidewalks, bumping into merchants.

It was August in the year A.D. 79. Pompeii went about its usual business of catering to the wealthy, of making money, of providing luxuries near the great mountain Vesuvius. At midday, just as the gold and silver dishes were being cleared away, the earth suddenly shook. The marble statues tottered, and the fine, designed plaster fell from ceilings. People ran into the streets, trying to escape the crumbling walls. Then, in a mighty clap, like the loudest thunder in the world, the top of Mount Vesuvius blew up. Fire and smoke and ash burst from it. Hot ash rained down on the people, who ran screaming for the ships in the harbor.

The sky, full of cinders and ash, made midnight at noon. Searing gas burned skin and lungs. Many people fell in the streets, and many died near the water. They died in their villas and in the bakeries. And then Vesuvius threw out tons and tons of ash which covered Pompeii to the rooftops. The city was lost. It lay buried and forgotten, this luxurious resort, for more than sixteen centuries. Then one day in the 1860s, workers discovered part of a building in the ancient place. Only lately have we come to know about the vast destruction the volcano caused.

The people of Pompeii probably believed as many Romans did that volcanoes burst up from the mighty forges of Vulcan, blacksmith of the gods. Today, scientists have other explanations for these massive eruptions. But both we and the Pompeiians would agree on one thing: volcanoes are beyond our control and our ability to predict.

INSIDE Information

In the late 1800s people came to Pompeii to dig up art or silver pieces to sell to museums. Most did not care what damage they did to buildings or objects they did not want.

A young Italian archeologist named Giuseppe Fiorelli kept Pompeii from being completely looted and destroyed by treasure hunters. He had a railroad built to carry away rubble and drew out careful maps to go by in clearing the old city. His cautious uncovering of the city revealed that the ash had preserved in detail the life of Pompeii. The paintings on the walls were still bright; loaves of bread remained in the ovens; bronze helmets and gold oil lamps gleamed like new. Why do you think things had been so well preserved?

Perhaps most telling of all, Fiorelli discovered holes left in the ash by the bodies that had decayed. He had the holes filled with plaster. When the ash was cleared, the forms of the Pompeiians remained, showing how the people had appeared at the moment of death.

Theories About Volcanic Activity

Beneath your feet right now, perhaps about 20 miles (32.18 km) down, is a slowly undulating sea of semiliquid rock. It moves and seethes all the time. Do you remember how some scientists think that this movement causes earthquakes? We rarely think of what goes on under the earth's crust. That is, not until some of the red-hot rock belches out onto the surface and runs and oozes over the land, scorching and burying everything in its path.

Some scientists believe that the inner core of the earth is solid because the pressure on it is so great. In the mantle of the earth, where the pressure is less great, the hot rock becomes more like a fluid or a thick plastic. Large globules of this liquid rock, called *magma*, break loose at the top of the mantle and float outward, rising against weak places in the earth's crust. When such masses reach a crack, or *vent*, in the upper mantle and crust, a volcano may form.

Other scientists believe that the plates of the earth's crust sliding over the mantle form magma between them and the mantle. Since almost all volcanoes occur along fault lines, the tremendous pressure between the plates may also heat rock to the melting point. The magma escapes or is forced out as the plates shift against each other.

Classification of Volcanoes

You may think that only peaked, sloping mountains that smoke and rumble are real volcanoes. But any of the places where molten rock comes to the surface–whether in a violent explosion or in a steady seeping–are called volcanoes. The mountains or *cones* that sometimes form around such openings are also called volcanoes. Many times volcanoes are classified by how they look on the surface–and how they look depends on how they erupt.

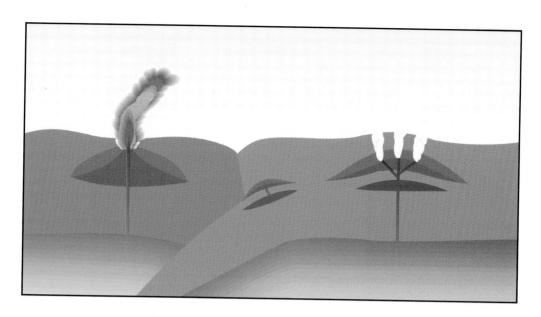

Kinds of Eruptions

Much of a volcano's force depends on how much gas is in the magma. Suppose you shook a bottle of warm, unopened soft drink. What would happen? What would happen when you opened the lid? There would be a "pop" and a gushing of foamy liquid. Why? This reaction depends on the amount of gas trapped in the drink. Now suppose you shook a bottle of "flat" soft drink. How would it sound when you loosened the cap? You would probably hear only a quiet fizz as the small amount of gas escaped.

Gases that are trapped in magma cannot always escape at the same rate. Have you ever watched pudding as it cooked? As it begins to get thick, it makes big, slow bubbles that rise and sink, sometimes without breaking. The hotter the pudding gets, the more bubbles form and break, popping and splattering. How is the boiling pudding different from boiling water? What do you think makes the difference? The thickness of the matter causes the difference. Gases escape easily from water. But in the thicker pudding, they are trapped briefly and then escape more explosively. What kind of magma do you think holds the most gases?

If a hole in the earth's crust is not blocked and the magma is runny, there will probably be no explosion, just a rather moderate gushing of *lava,* as magma that spills onto the earth's surface is called. Do you think this kind of volcano has magma that traps a lot of gases? Such eruptions are called *Hawaiian.* If the magma is thick, the volcano spits and sputters, throwing out cinders and steam. If the magma is so thick that it builds up pressure and explodes deep inside the volcano, magma, ash, and steam shoot out of the vent like a bullet out of a gun. Mount Vesuvius buried Pompeii in this kind of explosion, known as a *Vulcanian* eruption.

What do you think happens when the magma builds up pressure against a blocked vent? Sometimes, with a deafening roar, a whole mountain blows apart, sending out hot gas, burning ash, and rivers of glowing lava. Such an explosion occurred in Indonesia in 1883. A small island there called Krakatoa literally blew up, blasting rock and fire 50 miles into the air. The mountain, nearly 3,600 feet (1.097 km) tall, was entirely demolished. People 3,000 miles (4,827 km) away heard the boom four hours later. About 5 cubic miles of material went into the air that day, keeping everything within 50 miles (80.45 km) in total darkness for more than two days. For a year after, the glassy dust particles stayed high in the atmosphere and spread around the world, making spectacular sunsets as far away as England and the United States.

The most explosive volcanic eruptions are named *Pelean,* after Mount Pelée, a volcano that wiped an entire city off the earth. What makes this eruption different from the Vulcanian one is the heavy gas cloud that pours out and rolls down like lava. When Mount Pelée exploded in 1902, an avalanche of red-hot dust and gases bowled down the mountain into the sea, with more power and speed than a hurricane. In two minutes a city of 30,000 vanished forever. Where just moments before had been streets and carts and shops and people were now smoldering, flattened buildings and utter silence.

Shapes of Volcanoes

Most of the volcanoes in Hawaii have wide, gradually sloping sides. What kind of eruption do you think causes such a cone to form? Nonviolent pouring of lava allows the long slopes to build up. Many people think that these cones look like warriors' shields; so the form has become known as a *shield* volcano. The state of Hawaii grew out of the sea. As volcanoes erupted on the seafloor, the lava built up, time after time. Finally the cones came above the surface of the water–the islands of Hawaii. When volcanoes spread more lava on the islands now, the lava hardens and then weathers into soil, enriching the fields.

Recently, another island rose out of the sea, near Iceland. On November 15, 1963, Surtsey appeared as a long ridge, tossing out black clouds of ash and lava. By the next day, the island was 200 feet (60.96 m) high and 2,000 feet (609.6 m) long. Four months later, Surtsey was 500 feet (152.4 km) high and more than a mile (1.609 km) long. A steady flow of lava surged up and coated the island, flowing down into the sea and warming the water for hundreds of yards around. The lava poured forth over the next two and a half years, hardening and thus preserving the new island from being torn down by the ocean waves. Some people think it took millions of years for the islands of Hawaii to form, since Mauna Loa is one of the biggest mountains on earth. How do you think Surtsey's rising from 425 feet (129.54 m) under the ocean in three years affects theories about the age of Hawaii? Why do you think that volcanoes erupting under the water are usually quiet? The pressure and temperature of the water contain and cool the hot rock.

The more famous volcanoes are shaped like cones. These cones, made of cinders, are–not surprisingly–called *cinder cones*. What kind of eruption do you think forms cinder cones? Their sides rise at steeper angles than the sides of shield volcanoes, and they usually have a basin at the top called a *caldera*. Calderas are formed when volcanoes blast out great amounts of magma, emptying a hollow under the top of the mountain. Then the top of the mountain collapses as the lava cools, making a huge crater with steep sides. In 1903, one of the first scientists to look into a newly formed caldera said that it looked like a huge pit and sounded like a giant, roaring furnace. He said that deep inside he heard a terrible cracking that seemed to be rocks splitting apart. Over the caldera he saw a shimmery veil caused by the tremendous heat rising up.

Some volcanoes erupt quietly at times and explosively at times. The cones around such volcanoes are made of different layers of lava and cinder. These *composite cones* make some of the most beautiful mountains in the world. Mount Mayon in the Philippines is called the most nearly perfect volcanic cone.

Rates of Eruptions

Volcanoes can also be classified by the pace of their activity. A volcano that has erupted recently (in the last 100 years or so) is called *active*. A volcano that has not erupted for a long time but rumbles or steams occasionally is considered *dormant*. A volcano that has neither erupted nor shown any signs of activity for hundreds of years is an *extinct* volcano. Scientists think that such volcanoes will not erupt again, but no one can really say for sure. Many scientists now call volcanoes either active or dormant, not believing any volcano is truly extinct.

Finding Out . . .

About Volcanic Eruptions

1. Get some modeling clay, some baking soda, some vinegar, red and yellow food coloring, some tempera paints, and an old plastic dishpan or some newspapers.

2. Use modeling clay to form a volcano cone. Make a few ridges on the slopes and a crater in the top. Paint the outside of the cone to indicate the amount and position of vegetation. Let the paint dry.

3. Put the finished cone into the dishpan or on the newspapers. Fill the crater with baking soda. Tint the soda with a few drops of yellow and red food coloring. Pour some vinegar into the soda. What kind of eruption occurs? Would you say the "lava" has much or little gas trapped in it? Why?

What Comes out of Volcanoes

Everyone knows that volcanoes are vast forces of destruction. But people sometimes forget that volcanoes are also one of the most important means of building mountains and changing soils and landscapes. People choose to live near volcanoes, despite the dangers, because the minerals from lava make rich farmland. When lava spurts out onto the surface of the earth, it can form several kinds of rock, depending on what the magma was made of and on how quickly it cools.

pumice   obsidian   rhyolite

The faster the lava cools, the smoother the rock formed will be. Two different volcanic rocks can come from the same kind of magma that solidified in different ways. *Rhyolite,* a fine-grained rock, and *obsidian,* a glassy rock, both develop from the same kind of magma. Which rock do you think cooled more quickly? The obsidian did, as its shiny smoothness shows. Because of its beauty, obsidian has been used in jewelry for hundreds of years. When the foam from the top of boiling lava cools swiftly, it forms a rock full of holes called *pumice,* a stone so light that it will float in water. Why do you think pumice has the texture it does?

Volcanoes can also produce tons of ash and solid fragments collectively called *tephra.* Some volcanoes throw out mostly tephra; others mostly lava. What volcano have you read about that buried a city under tephra? Where do you think you would find volcanoes producing mostly lava?

The products of volcanoes deadliest to human life are the gases. The mixture of hot gases and fine dust travels much like a fluid. The worst disaster from volcanic gases happened in the Mount Pelée eruption of 1902. The cloud of superheated steam and fiery particles rolled over Saint Pierre, killing all but one of its citizens. The heat of the volcano was so strong that no one could come ashore from ships to look for survivors. When a search party did come three days later, they found a prisoner in a cell with only one tiny window. He was badly burned, but he recovered and became somewhat famous telling his story. Why do you think his cell helped him survive?

The main gas in magma and lava is steam. It is the steam that causes magma to be explosive. When water changes to steam, its volume increases one thousand times. The heat of molten rock can change water to steam instantly. What do you think happens when water meets magma deep under ground where the steam cannot escape? The water remains water, but gets much hotter than it ever could on the earth's surface. Then when the water reaches a place where the pressure on it is not so great, it turns to steam in a sudden, powerful blast. The noise volcanoes make results from the massive release of vapor particles that takes place when the water all at once occupies one thousand times more room than it did one second earlier.

Most volcanoes smell like rotten eggs, indicating that sulfur is also present in the magma. Other gases found in magma are carbon dioxide, hydrogen, and carbon monoxide. Even with the most modern equipment, collectors find it hard to get gas samples from erupting volcanoes. Besides the difficulty of getting to the vent, the collectors cannot keep from collecting gases from the atmosphere along with the volcanic gases. Why would they want to keep atmospheric gases out?

Finding Out . . .

About Lava

1. Get some white sugar, some margarine, some water, some food coloring, a metal pan, a glass beaker, a hot plate (or be able to use a stove), a wooden spoon, some wax paper, a candy thermometer, a measuring cup, and three ovenproof dishes.

2. Watch as your teacher mixes and heats some ingredients. When your teacher tells you, bring the beaker filled with cold water to the stove or hot plate. Drop a few drops of the hot mixture into the water. Record what happens.

3. Let some of the mixture cool slowly in the ovenproof dishes. How does it differ from the mixture that cooled in the water? Whip some of the remaining mixture with the spoon. Drop some into water. Let some cool slowly. How are they different? Record all your observations.

How Volcanoes Influence the Weather

Benjamin Franklin once theorized that ash and dust from volcanoes could affect the weather. When the summer of 1783 had been unusually cold in Paris, Franklin said perhaps the volcano erupting in Iceland was the cause. No one really thought he could be on the right track.

Scientists have recently come to understand that the mighty furnaces of the earth do affect our weather. The year 1816 has been called "the year with no summer." All over the world, the temperatures were unusually cold all year long. In the northeastern United States, for example, there was snow in the middle of June and killing frosts every month. What effect do you think this weather had on crops? Crops failed, and food was scarce in many places that year. The year before, the volcano Tambora had thrown out several cubic miles of ash and gas. The finest dust and much of the gas went high into the stratosphere and spread around the world several times. Most scientists think that that one volcanic eruption was enough to account for the "year with no summer."

Why do you think that volcanoes erupting can make the earth colder? Some people thought that the dust in the air blocked the sunlight. But after tracking volcanic products in the atmosphere with weather satellites, scientists have concluded that it is not how much a volcano puts out, but *what* it puts out. Sulfurous gases can rise much higher than dust and ash. In about six months, dust and ash have been washed out of the air. But the gases, above the rain, become clouds that may absorb sunlight. Every year around fifty volcanoes erupt. Although few are as dramatic as Krakatoa and Tambora, their combined products must certainly influence our skies.

Other Kinds of Eruptions:
Hot Springs

In several places around the world, bubbling hot water comes to the surface and collects in pools. Many scientists think that the water is partly surface water and partly underground water that is heated by magma close to the surface of the earth. The warm water brews up, kept warm by new hot water always coming in.

In many countries, such as Germany and Iceland, people visit the springs for the comfort their mineral waters seem to bring. Some say that soaking in the springs helps stop the pains of arthritis and other diseases. Some places also use the steady supply of hot water to heat hospitals, schools, greenhouses, and swimming pools. Scientists are also trying to find ways to use the hot underground water to generate electricity.

Some hot springs in Japan have iron compounds in them, making the water a deep red. A few such springs have water so hot that the government has put up fences to keep people from falling in and burning themselves. In many places in the city of Beppu, springs bubble up along roadsides, forming little pools hot enough for people to boil eggs.

Perhaps you have been to Yellowstone National Park in the western United States. Even if you have not, you have probably heard of Old Faithful, a hole in the ground that regularly spouts forth steam and water. It is a *geyser,* a hot spring with fountain action. *Geyser* comes from the Icelandic word meaning "to gush." When water is under pressure and heated beyond the normal boiling point, it will escape explosively at the first opportunity.

Geysers have much in common with volcanoes. For one thing, they almost always occur in the same regions as volcanoes and earthquakes. For another, their spoutings, although comparatively mild, are indeed eruptions. How are geyser eruptions and volcanic eruptions alike?

Finding Out . . .

About Geysers

1. Get a large funnel, a Pyrex beaker or a pan, some water, and a hot plate (or be able to use a stove).

2. Put the wide end of the funnel in the beaker, and put water in the beaker until it becomes level with the stem of the funnel.

3. Place the beaker over heat. What happens when the water begins to boil? How do you think geysers spout?

Recent Eruptions

Mount Redoubt

In late 1989 and early 1990, a large volcano in Alaska called Mount Redoubt began to toss cinders and dust high into the air. The flying ash was thick enough to clog the engines of airplanes, causing several crashes. The Anchorage airport had to shut down temporarily. Scientists settled in to watch and record the activity. Just a few years earlier, another mountain to the south had rumbled to life, and scientists there had a front seat at a major eruption.

Mount St. Helens

In the early spring of 1980, a few rumblings disturbed the peaceful land around Mount St. Helens in Washington. A little ash puffed out and dusted the top of the mountain. The mountain began to form a huge bulge on one side, and the summit cracked open in several places. Scientists monitored the volcano carefully, and after earthquakes shook the area several times, the experts agreed: Mount St. Helens was going to erupt. Everyone was warned to leave the area and to stay out.

Almost everyone heeded the warning. A few seismologists and volcanologists stationed themselves at what seemed safe distances from the smouldering peak, and photographers and reporters took up vantage points to wait. The mountain seemed to wait too, its snowy and forested sides beautiful in the sunlight.

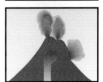

Then on May 18, at 8:32 in the morning, there was a sudden earthquake, and the whole north side of Mount St. Helens blew out. A rush of steam went skyward, followed by a dark cloud of ash that roared out and up. The blast was 500 times greater than the atomic bomb dropped on Japan in World War II. It blew the top of the mountain into powder and threw more than a cubic mile of mountain into the stratosphere. The 200-mile-an-hour (321.8-km) winds ripped trees out by the roots and flattened whole forests for 15 miles (24.14 km). The hot gas and ash poured down on top of the destruction; a hot mud flooded rivers and lakes. Then a thick coating of gray ash settled over everything, and more ash drifted east. By evening, Mount St. Helens, 3,000 feet (914.4 m) shorter now on the north, sent up a single plume of fine dust and steam.

For miles around, the blanket of ash had turned the once lush region into a barren, colorless landscape, resembling the surface of some desolate planet. But in less than two months, green plants were pushing through the cover, flowers were blooming again, and animals were returning. The place, though different, was coming back to life, renewed and fresh. Trees are growing there now; the waters are clear; the place is green. God has designed the earth to renew itself. What seems utter destruction to us is part of the mighty plan of the Creator for the continuing of life.

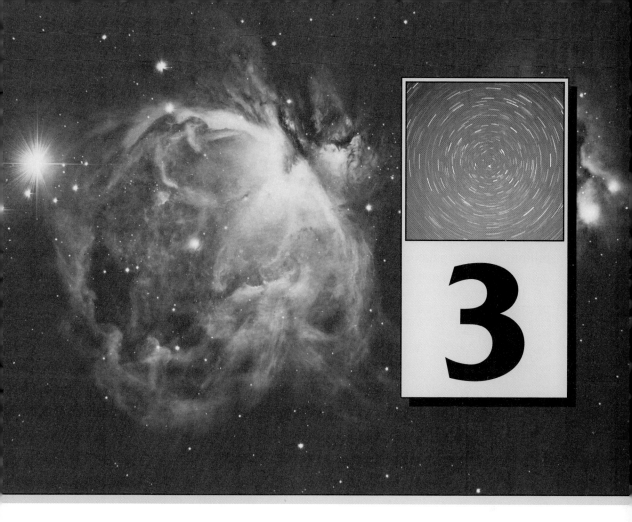

 **Stars**

"And he brought him forth abroad, and said, Look now toward heaven, and tell the stars, if thou be able to number them."

Genesis 15:5

How many stars do you think there are? Two hundred million? A billion? A quintillion? There are more stars in the universe than we can even imagine, much less count. The latest guess is that there are more than 100 billion stars in our home galaxy alone, and there are billions and billions of other galaxies. And there may be billions more galaxies that we have not yet detected.

The Stars

If you glance up on a clear night, you can easily notice a few hundred stars. If you watch them for a moment, you will see that they appear to twinkle. If you study them carefully, you will begin to observe even more: some stars seem bigger than others, some are red, others are blue-white, and some are far brighter than others. Do you think stars are all different from each other, or do you think your eyes are playing tricks on you?

Magnitude

"There is one glory of the sun, and another glory of the moon, and another glory of the stars: for one star differeth from another star in glory."

I Corinthians 15:41

All stars are enormous balls of gas producing their own light. The main ingredient in a star is hydrogen. When the hydrogen atoms in the center of the star become heated to millions of degrees and are crushed under the weight of the star, they are changed into helium. Millions of these changes, or nuclear reactions, take place every second in the center of every star, generating tremendous amounts of heat and light. Why do you think some stars make more light than others?

How bright a star looks to us depends upon its distance from Earth, its size, and its temperature. Our sun appears bright because it is close to Earth compared to other stars that are hundreds or millions of light-years away. The farther away a star is, the bigger or brighter it must be in order for us to see it. The star named Betelgeuse looks smaller than our sun because it is 527 light-years from Earth; but it is so large that if it were where our sun is, it would fill up our solar system past the orbit of Mars. How do you think our sun would look from Betelgeuse?

Betelgeuse

absolute

apparent

absolute

apparent

Scientists categorize stars into three main sizes: *dwarf, giant,* and *supergiant.* Some scientists recognize *super-supergiants* as well. A dwarf star is any star of average or small size. Our sun is classified as a dwarf. Giant stars are large and hundreds of thousands of times brighter than the sun. Supergiants are hundreds of times larger than the sun and are as much as a million times brighter. Betelgeuse is a supergiant. A star like VV Cephei (cē'fē) could be called a super-supergiant. If it were placed where our sun is, it would take up not only Mars' orbit but also Jupiter's.

We refer to the brightness of stars as seen from Earth as *apparent magnitude.* The phrase refers to how great the star appears to be. How bright the star actually shines is called its *absolute magnitude.* Imagine that you see an ordinary living-room lamp from a block away. It would probably seem about as bright as a candle. Its apparent magnitude would be rather faint. But if someone carried the lamp toward you, it would get brighter and larger. Were the lamp right in front of you, you could tell exactly how bright it was.

If all the stars were the same distance away from us, we could immediately tell which were the brightest and biggest. They would not just look brighter; they would *be* brighter. Hipparchus, a Greek who lived shortly before the time Christ was on earth, devised a system to classify stars by their brightness. The brightest stars on this scale are first-magnitude (+1) stars. Sixth-magnitude (+6) stars are the faintest we can see without a telescope.

When we speak of the magnitude of a star, we must be sure to make it clear whether we mean absolute or apparent magnitude. Now we rank stars into the negative numbers. Rigel, for example, a blue-white star, has an absolute magnitude of -7. Is Rigel brighter or dimmer than a +1 star? It is far brighter. It has an apparent magnitude of 0. Do you think Rigel is brighter or dimmer than Betelgeuse? Betelgeuse has an absolute magnitude of -5.6, and its apparent magnitude is +0.4. Telescopes also let us see smaller stars and stars farther away; so the scale was expanded on the other end as well–to +23. It takes a strong telescope to detect a star with a magnitude in the twenties.

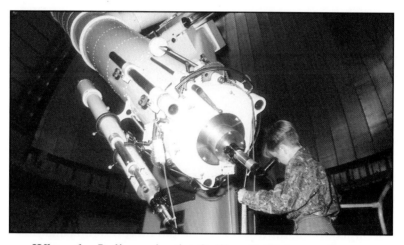

When the Italian scientist Galileo Galilei turned a telescope toward the sky in 1610, he saw thousands and thousands of stars that no one in his day suspected were there. How do you think telescopes changed beliefs about stars? No longer did it seem possible to count the stars. And the familiar stars showed themselves to be brighter and bigger than they had seemed before. After telescopes were invented, Hipparchus's scale had to be expanded. Can you guess why? Would Hipparchus have been classifying the apparent magnitude or the absolute magnitude of stars? The apparent magnitude. Telescopes showed that the scale was not sufficient for absolute magnitudes.

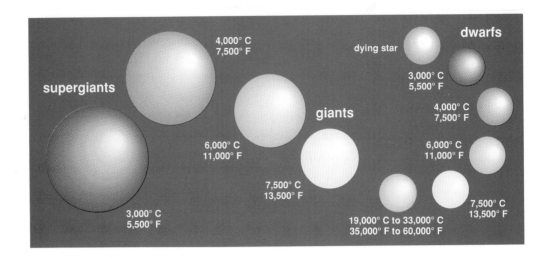

A star's brightness also depends on its temperature. The hottest stars, with surface temperatures of 35,000 to 60,000° F (19,000 to 33,000° C), are blue-white or white. Yellow stars are about 11,800° F (6,000° C). Orange stars are about 7,500° F (4,000° C), and red stars, the "coolest," have a temperature of about 5,500° F (3,000° C). About how hot do you think our sun is? Which stars do you think shine the most brilliantly, all other things being equal? The hottest stars shine the brightest. Think of the living-room lamps again. If two three-way lamps exactly the same size are side by side, the one that has been turned to the third level will shine more brightly than the one turned only to the first level.

Special Kinds of Stars

The brightness of a star is not necessarily constant. There are stars that flare up brightly, grow dimmer, and flare up again. These are called *variable stars*. Scientists theorize that these stars explode, grow larger, and then shrink, time after time. Some expand and contract with clockwork regularity. The star Eta has a bright-to-dim period of seven days, four hours, and fourteen minutes. Others are completely unpredictable; Ras Algethi grows twice as bright at times, but no one has been able to find any pattern in its fluctuations.

Scientists theorize that as a star's nuclear reactions begin to slow down, it shrinks inward because there is not enough pressure in the core to hold up the outer star. The helium core draws inward under its own weight, and the temperature rises again. When it has risen to 180,000,000° F (100,000,000° C), nuclear reactions may increase, releasing energy and thus enabling the star to return to a stable state. It is possible, though, that instead of becoming stable, the star will continue contracting and expanding. Some other variable stars result from two stars revolving around each other, sometimes sharing their brightness and sometimes blocking each other out.

Sometimes a star suddenly grows hundreds or even thousands of times brighter and then fades to far less than it was to begin with, never to brighten again. In the past when such a phenomenon lit the skies, many regarded it as a bad sign, as a mark of disorder in the heavens. Some believed that it signaled the birth of a star. Astronomers called such a star a *nova,* which means "new." Since a nova usually brightens a star that was not visible to the naked eye before, sky watchers thought they were seeing a star "born."

Now we know that the mighty flare is the explosive end of a star. When a star "goes nova," scientists believe that its core, depleted of fuel, collapses. The star actually falls in on itself and then flashes outward, finishing in a supreme blaze of glory. Because its energy is spread out, and therefore not as intense as it was, the surface temperature of the star drops to about 5,432° F (3,000° C). What color do you think the star becomes? It can still be from 100 to 10,000 times brighter than the sun. How can that be? The star is cooler but much bigger than the sun. Unusually bright novas, sometimes brighter than a whole galaxy, are called *supernovas*. A supernova is as different from a nova as dynamite is different from a sparkler. A supernova may flare up for several weeks, hurling gases into space that will be visible by telescope for centuries.

INSIDE Information

Can we say that stars die? Scientists believe that stars end their existence as *white dwarfs,* dim stars only about the size of the earth. When no new energy is being produced, the star slowly contracts. All the particles of star material draw closer and closer together, becoming far denser than any substance on earth. The collapse will stop only when the atomic particles are squeezed as tightly together as they can be. A teaspoonful of such material might weigh several tons on earth.

Sometimes when stars suddenly collapse, the atoms are not just pushed together; they are actually forced to combine. This reaction produces a *dense star*. These incredibly dense bodies emit regular pulses of energy every second. Only stars many times more massive than our sun can become dense stars. Because the energy these stars produce is radioactive, the term *radio star* or *pulsar* may also be applied to them. But there is a final stage more mysterious yet, reserved for the biggest stars.

When the most massive of stars collapse, scientists theorize that the matter in their cores is crushed until only an intense field of gravity remains. The gravity is so strong that nothing in the area can escape its pull. Light itself is sucked into what is called a *black hole*. Do you think anyone has ever seen a black hole? Why not?

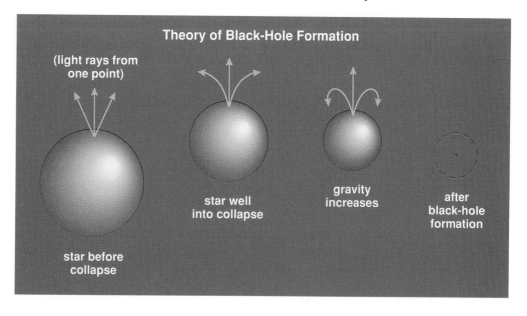

Theory of Black-Hole Formation

(light rays from one point)

star before collapse

star well into collapse

gravity increases

after black-hole formation

Although black holes are invisible, scientists are fairly certain that they see the effects of them. One black hole seems to be partnered with a blue supergiant. Circling the star there seems to be an invisible object that attracts gases away from the star. The gases are sucked into the object, becoming so hot that they emit x-rays intense enough to be detected by instruments on Earth.

Why Stars Seem to Twinkle

1. Get a strong flashlight, a large magnifying glass, and an electric hot plate. You will also need a projection screen.

2. Shine the flashlight on the screen. Hold the magnifying glass so that the center of the glass is at the same height as the bulb of the flashlight. Focus the light on the screen. Darken the room. Describe what you see on the screen.

3. Place the hot plate in front of and just below the lens. Turn the hot plate on. What happens to the light image? If you think of the flashlight in your model as a star, what does the heat from the hot plate represent? What can you say about the effect of Earth's atmosphere on how the stars look to us?

Groups of Stars

If we could travel along at millions of times the speed of light, we might be able to tour a small corner of the universe in a lifetime. We would, of course, never live long enough or be able to travel fast enough to see it all. But suppose we could see some of the sights out there firsthand; what do you think we might see? Do you think it would be just vast emptiness with a star blazing by every few light-years?

Stars do not always burn in isolated glory. Some spin through space in pairs. These *binary stars* revolve around each other, held together by their pull on each other. Do you remember how some scientists think binary stars explain changes in magnitude? Sometimes many stars are bound together, forming a *star cluster*. Possibly the most famous cluster is *Pleiades*. Although it is often called the *Seven Sisters,* there are far more than seven stars in the cluster. Large telescopes have shown it has more than 500 stars, many surrounded by clouds of shining gases. Even bigger groups, called *globular clusters,* have as many as 100,000 stars in them. All of these groups of stars are held together by their pull on each other.

Our star, which we call the sun, does not have companion stars, but it has companions–the planets. A *solar system* is a star and a group of planets and asteroids that circle in orbit around that star. Do any other single stars have planets around them? We do not know. Planets are too cold to send out enough of their own light for us to see them. We can see planets only as they reflect the light from their star. The nearest star to us is too far away for us to see a planet reflecting light, even with our strongest telescopes. But some observers believe that many of the stars we see may have planets around them.

The space between stars is often swirling with many clouds of dust and gas, called *nebulae*. One dark cloud, the Horsehead Nebula, wavers in brilliant reds and blues because of the way starlight shines on the dust and gas particles in it. An exploding star often makes a cloud of dust called a *circumstellar cloud. Circumstellar* comes from words meaning "around a star." *Interstellar* ("between the stars") clouds are made of dust and gases drifting in the empty areas of space. With the help of special telescopes, we can see into these clouds that are too bright for ordinary telescopes. Some scientists believe that new stars are "born" from these clouds. They think that the grains of dust sometimes begin to pull together, eventually making a star. Since no one has ever seen this happening, what must we say about the idea? It is a theory, not a scientific fact.

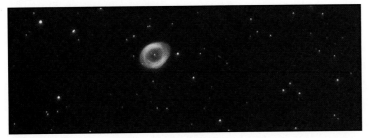

Galaxies

Billions of stars seem to travel together in space, in huge groups called *galaxies*. A *galaxy* is a collection of stars, dust, and gases, all held together by the pull of gravity. If you look as far out into space as you can, you are looking at the galaxy to which the sun and the solar system belong. It is called simply *The Galaxy*. Part of it, called the *Milky Way,* is the broad band of light stretching across the sky each night. The distance across it is about 100,000 light-years. The expanse of our own galaxy is almost more than we can comprehend. Then we remember that there are billions of other galaxies, each holding millions and millions of stars spaced light-years apart. The universe is immense beyond our imagination. Yet God created all with a word and oversees it all with a glance. The more man learns about space, the more amazing his Creator's power becomes to him and the more limited his own knowledge and abilities must appear.

Our Galaxy is shaped roughly like a wheel. It is one of many *spiral* galaxies, collections of stars that spin like a pinwheel. These galaxies are thickest toward the center with thinning arms swirling outward. From overhead such galaxies look something like the design in a huge lollipop. From the side they look like a fried egg. Another kind of galaxy, the *elliptical* galaxy, is more of a disc than a spiral, like a plate. Another kind is the *starburst* galaxy. This kind seems to be a ball of stars nearly the same density throughout. In the past few years, observers have discovered that there are dozens of kinds of galaxies, even some that seem to be in a category all by themselves. And galaxies exist in all sizes, from *supergalaxies* to *dwarfs*.

Observers have also discovered that galaxies, like stars, come in pairs and groups and clusters. Our own galaxy is one of the larger members of the cluster we call the *Local Group*. This supersystem contains eighteen or twenty galaxies and may be 2,000,000 light-years wide. Another group, sometimes called *Stephan's Quintet* and sometimes *Stephan's Quartet,* contains just four or five galaxies. Do you think that all galaxies in a group are the same kind? No, a cluster may contain many kinds, although usually one kind will dominate. Scientists now think that clusters of clusters, *superclusters,* may exist. One such collection seems to be a neighborhood of several clusters, containing hundreds of galaxies. Yet in all that observers have been able to see, there is no center, no dense middle, in the vastness of the universe.

"Canst thou bind the sweet influences of Pleiades, or loose the bands of Orion?"

Job 38:31

The Constellations

Night after night, for generation upon generation, the stars have made the same patterns in our skies. We call the patterns, the groups that stars seem to form, *constellations.* Centuries ago watchers of the sky began naming constellations after the pictures they had imagined in them. Perhaps you have done something similar, looking up at passing clouds, seeing animals or cars or faces in them. The *astronomers,* people who study things outside the earth, named the constellations after gods, folk heroes, animals, and objects. It takes some imagination to see how most constellations got their names.

Before you try to find the constellations in the sky, it helps to see drawings of them with the figures they are named for outlined around them. As you can see in the pictures, constellations are not like dot-to-dot drawings. They are more like a few posts on which great tents are hung. After you look at several drawings, you can venture out to find the real things overhead.

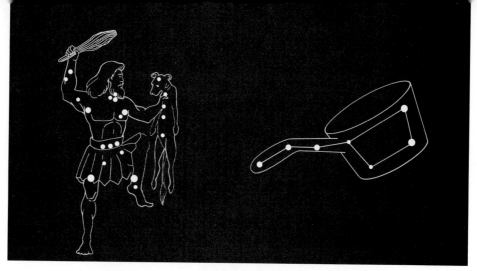

When you view the night sky, keep in mind that particular constellations will be clearly visible only at certain times of the year. You can easily see the Big Dipper, for instance, in the summer; Orion and Pleiades in the winter. If you keep track of the constellations through the months, you will see that they appear to revolve slowly, returning to their original positions in a year. Why do you think that the constellations change with the seasons? They seem to move because the earth has orbited around the sun during that time. A good guide book will tell you what times of year each constellation shows up best and will give you pictures and tips for finding your way around the night sky.

Once you find one constellation, you can use it to help you find others. The Big Dipper can direct you to the North Star and the Little Dipper and from there to Cassiopeia. The two stars on the outside of the cup of the Big Dipper (called "pointers") point to the North Star. The North Star is the first star in the handle of the Little Dipper. The star nearest the cup in the handle of the Big Dipper and the North Star guide you to the middle star of Cassiopeia. If you find the three almost evenly spaced jewels of Orion's "belt," you can find the star Sirius and the Pleiades. A line to the left through the belt shows you Sirius; a slightly curving line to the right directs you toward the Pleiades.

"Seek him that maketh the seven stars and Orion."

Amos 5:8

Some Northern Constellations of Summer

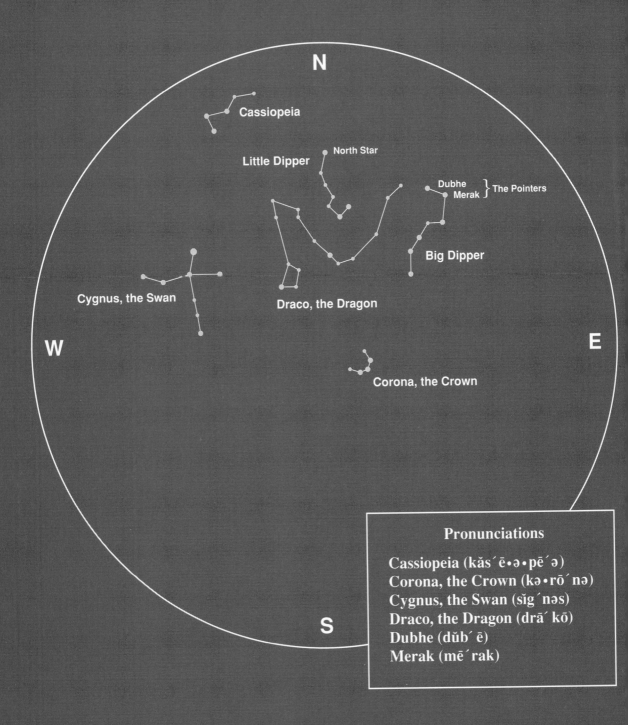

Pronunciations

Cassiopeia (kăs´ē•ə•pē´ə)
Corona, the Crown (kə•rō´nə)
Cygnus, the Swan (sĭg´nəs)
Draco, the Dragon (drā´kō)
Dubhe (dŭb´ē)
Merak (mē´rak)

Some Northern Constellations of Winter

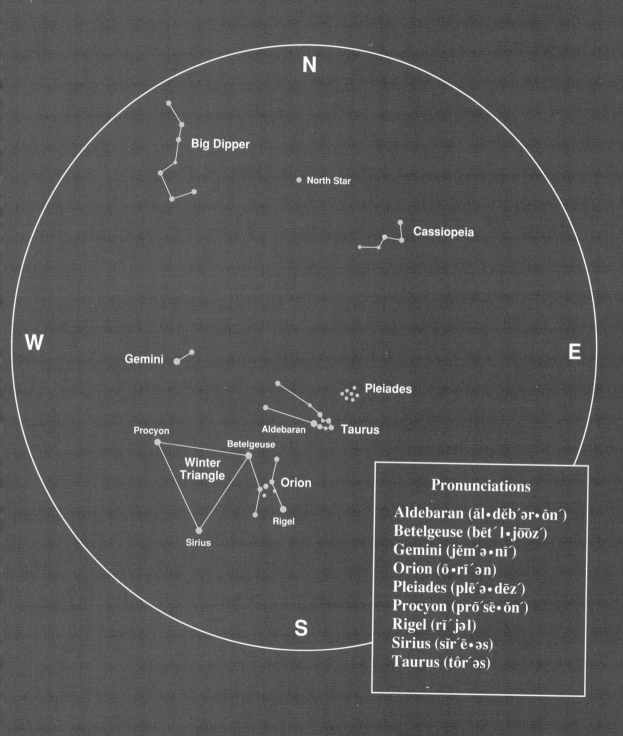

Big Dipper

North Star

Cassiopeia

Gemini

Pleiades

Procyon

Aldebaran

Taurus

Betelgeuse

Winter
Triangle

Orion

Rigel

Sirius

N

W

E

S

Pronunciations

Aldebaran (ăl•děb´ər•ŏn´)
Betelgeuse (bēt´l•jōōz´)
Gemini (jĕm´ə•nī´)
Orion (ō•rī´ən)
Pleiades (plē´ə•dēz´)
Procyon (prō´sē•ŏn´)
Rigel (rī´jəl)
Sirius (sĭr´ē•əs)
Taurus (tôr´əs)

Finding Out . . .

About Orion and the Big Dipper

1. Get your notebook, a flashlight, and–if possible–a pair of binoculars. Choose a night when there are no clouds and the moon is not full.

2. Before you go out, study the diagrams of the constellations in your notebook. Then go outside. Try to find a place where there are no bright streetlights to interfere with your view. Look over the sky until you see the three stars in Orion's belt or the handle of the Big Dipper.

3. Without looking at your notebook page, try to find Orion's shoulders, his legs, and his face. Can you see the string of stars that form the animal skin he carries in his left hand? Or, if you find the Big Dipper handle, find the cup of the dipper. Can you find the North Star, using the two stars on the outside of the cup as guides? Use the binoculars to look more closely at some of the stars. How do they look different from when you view them without the glasses?

4. Mark the stars you found. Can you name any of them?

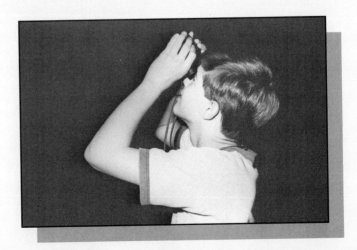

About Other Constellations

1. Get several empty 12-ounce soft-drink cans, a finishing nail, a two-penny nail, a hammer, your notebook, some blank labels, and a pen.

2. Using the patterns in your notebook, punch holes in the bottom of the soft-drink cans with the nails. Use one can for each different constellation. Label each can with the name of the constellation it represents.

3. Hold a can up to the light and look through the tab opening. Can you recognize the constellation? Keep a record of how many constellations you can name without looking at the labels.

Finding Out . . .

About How Constellations Move

1. Get an old black umbrella, some washable white fabric paint or some hem chalk, your notebook, and a ruler.

2. With your teacher's help, use the diagrams from your notebook to draw constellations on the inside of the open umbrella. Use your ruler to get the distances correct.

3. Hold the umbrella over your head. Look at the summer constellations. Without moving your eyes, turn the umbrella slowly to the winter constellations. Have someone hold the umbrella still while you slowly turn under it, looking up. Which way of viewing the drawn constellations do you think is most like the way the constellations change in our skies? Why?

You may have heard some of the constellations referred to as part of the *zodiac*. The zodiac is a chart that represents the path of the sun, moon, planets, and stars across the sky. *Astrologers* are people who believe that the positions of stars and planets cause events on the earth or influence human beings to do certain things. They consult the zodiac to foretell events in a person's life. An astrologer is not an astronomer. How are they different? Which one is interested in observing and recording facts? Christians do not look to astrologers for guidance. They put their confidence in the sure Word of God and trust the Holy Spirit to lead them.

Measurement in Astronomy

"Is not God in the height of heaven? and behold the height of the stars, how high they are!"

Job 22:12

When you look at the constellations, the starlight you see has been traveling toward earth for many years before you see it. For example, the light you see from the star Alpha Centauri (the star closest to our sun) left on its journey four and a half years ago. If you are twelve now, you were only eight when that light was produced. All other stars are much farther away. Columbus was exploring the Americas when the light from some stars that will shine tonight was sent forth. The light from even more distant stars has been traveling toward the earth since before the Flood.

How do astronomers measure such vast distances? Here is a simple way to understand the method scientists use to measure the distance to a star. Hold one finger out at arm's length before your eyes. Close one eye and notice what objects that finger covers. Now open that eye and close the other. Does it seem as though the finger has shifted and is covering different objects? If you try this in front of a bookcase, you can count the number of books that "shifted." If you move the finger closer to your face and repeat the process, the shift will be bigger.

Astronomers call this shift *parallax*. The star whose distance is being calculated is the "finger" in the experiment. Instead of using their eyes to measure as you did, scientists take pictures six months apart in order to be at opposite points in the earth's orbit. These pictures are the "eyes." Scientists measure the shift of the nearby star compared with more distant stars. The greater the shift, the nearer the star.

Some scientists say that the universe is extremely old because we can see stars that are millions of light-years away. For us to see them, they argue, the light must have been traveling for millions of years. Is this necessarily true? No, the God who created all the stars in an instant by the breath of His mouth could easily have caused the light of those stars to be visible everywhere at once.

When scientists talk about the *Big Bang,* they mean the theory that the universe appeared in seconds, in a huge explosion, millions of years ago. Scientists who hold this theory agree that everything in existence came from that one incredible "bang" and that no one has observed any star or planet forming since then. But they refuse to recognize the Almighty Creator who in the beginning said, "Let there be light." They try to build bigger telescopes and put them higher on mountains or even into space to get a better view, hoping to find proof for their theory. All they will find, however, is that the stronger our telescopes become, and the more we see, the more we will stand in awe of God's omnipotence.

"He telleth the number of the stars; he calleth them all by their names."

Psalm 147:4

Space
Exploration

"Mine hand also hath laid the foundation of the earth, and my right hand hath spanned the heavens: when I call unto them, they stand up together."

Isaiah 48:13

Over one million people gathered at the Kennedy Space Center early on the morning of July 16, 1969. About 500 million others were looking at the scene on their televisions at home. For hours already the engineers had been checking and rechecking the spacecraft systems. The astronauts, their pulses quickening, waited in the ship. Then, at last, the engines were fired. All over the world, watchers chanted with the countdown: "5 . . . 4 . . . 3 . . . 2 . . . 1 . . . BLASTOFF!" With a mighty roar and trembling, *Apollo 11* churned upward, aiming three Americans toward the moon.

Just a couple hundred years ago, people said that the best way to get to the moon would be to tie big birds, like hawks, to a chair and let them fly you there. And even into the twentieth century, people were thinking up bizarre ways to get from the earth to the moon or Mars or another galaxy. It is just in the lifetime of your parents that men have been able to travel in space at all. In forty years, men advanced from small, simple rockets to ships that landed on the moon to shuttles that go and come from space as an airplane from an airport.

First Attempts

The Chinese were probably the first people to invent rockets, sometime in the 1200s. The rocket cases were probably made out of many layers of tightly wrapped paper coated with shellac and were set off with gunpowder. The Chinese used the ''arrows of flying fire'' as weapons to defend their capital city.

Several hundred years later, William Congreve in England made a rocket that would explode with great noise and glare when it was ignited. The words ''the rockets' red glare'' from the ''Star Spangled Banner'' are describing rockets such as Congreve designed. You can still see examples of these rockets in Fourth of July celebrations.

Then in the late 1880s, Robert Goddard, a seventeen-year-old in Massachusetts, sat looking at the stars. It suddenly occurred to him that it might be possible to build a rocket that would reach them. He told his mother that he would get one of those stars for her, and he spent the rest of his life experimenting with rockets.

Goddard decided to use liquid fuel, rather than the gunpowder used in the Chinese rockets. He worked for years, failing time after time. Finally in 1926, he managed to launch a rocket. It went only 41 feet (12.5 m) high and traveled 184 feet (56 m) at about 60 miles (96.5 km) an hour. But Robert made his rockets better and better–and by 1935 they could reach 7,500 feet (2,286 m) and travel over 700 miles (1,126.3 km) an hour.

For a rocket to go into orbit around Earth, however, it would have to reach a speed of 18,000 miles (29,000 km) per hour; and to leave Earth's orbit, it would have to fly at 25,000 miles (40,000 km) per hour. It would be difficult to build a rocket that could reach those speeds. What do you think are some of the problems in building such a rocket?

One problem is getting enough push, or *thrust,* to get away from Earth. When an airplane takes off, the burning fuel ejects gases out the back of the craft. The backward push of those gases against the air outside causes the airplane to go forward. A *propellant* is a fuel that provides the thrust. How do you think a rocket propellant needs to be different from an airplane propellant?

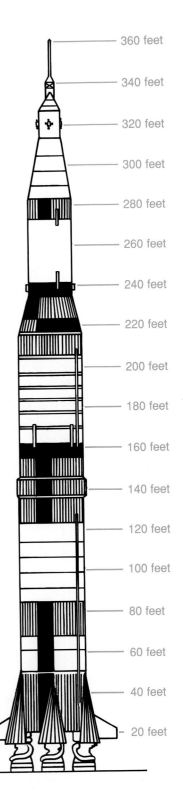

360 feet
340 feet
320 feet
300 feet
280 feet
260 feet
240 feet
220 feet
200 feet
180 feet
160 feet
140 feet
120 feet
100 feet
80 feet
60 feet
40 feet
20 feet

Goddard's 1926 rocket

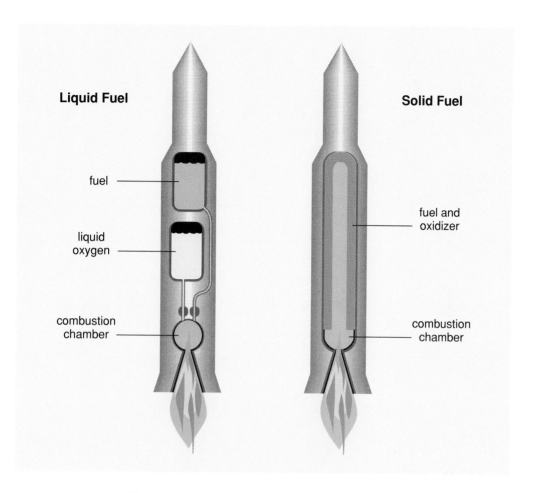

Liquid Fuel

fuel

liquid
oxygen

combustion
chamber

Solid Fuel

fuel and
oxidizer

combustion
chamber

But even if finding a propellant that would lift a rocket away from the earth were not difficult, there is yet another problem: lack of air. Air is important to airplane flight. The fuel in planes needs air in order to burn.

Unlike a plane that uses air to burn fuel, a rocket uses an *oxidizer,* a device that supplies the needed oxygen to burn the fuel. The oxidizer and the fuel together give the rocket its exploding thrust in takeoff.

Look at the diagram of the rocket. Where is the fuel burned? Why do you think the *combustion chamber* is placed where it is? How much space in the rocket is used for fuel? Why do you think so much of the rocket is needed to make thrust?

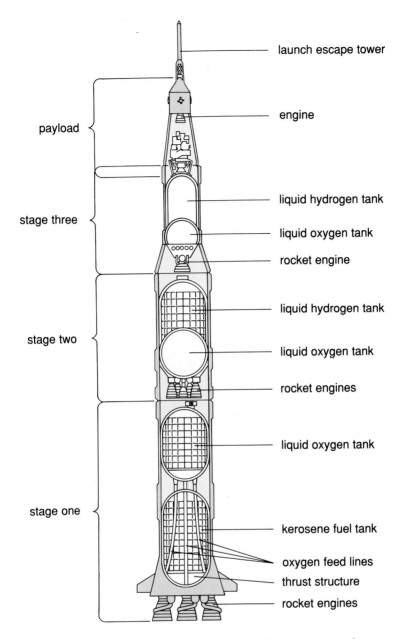

launch escape tower

engine

liquid hydrogen tank

liquid oxygen tank

rocket engine

liquid hydrogen tank

liquid oxygen tank

rocket engines

liquid oxygen tank

kerosene fuel tank

oxygen feed lines

thrust structure

rocket engines

payload

stage three

stage two

stage one

A rocket is really made up of two different parts: the *launch vehicle,* or rocket engine, and the *payload*. The payload contains the actual spacecraft–its instruments, crew, and life-support systems.

A *multistage* rocket has two or more separate engines and fuel tanks; each stage drops to the earth after its fuel is used. Why would a multistage rocket fly higher than a single-stage rocket?

68

Finding Out . . .

About Rocket Thrust

1. Get some nylon thread, a measuring tape or stick, a drinking straw, a small balloon, a large balloon, some masking tape, and your notebook.

2. Blow up the small balloon. Hold the end so that the air cannot escape. Tape the drinking straw to the side of the balloon. Slide the nylon thread through the straw. Tie the thread to a doorknob or some other steady object. Pull the balloon all the way to the other end of the thread. Hold the thread parallel to the floor. Draw the thread straight and tight.

3. Let go of the end of the balloon and watch what happens. Measure how far it traveled. Blow up the balloon again. This time hold the balloon near the floor. Let go of the balloon, being careful to note where it stops climbing. Measure how far it traveled.

4. Try the experiments with the large balloon. What differences do you notice? Try holding the thread in different positions. What happens?

Satellites

The Soviet Union is given credit for launching the world's first artificial satellite on October 4, 1957. It was called *Sputnik,* which is Russian for "traveling companion." America launched its first satellite, *Explorer 1,* on January 31, 1958. For the next twenty years, both countries raced to send faster and better machines into space.

Many of the first satellites gathered information about the earth. Some, such as TIROS (for *T*elevison and *I*nfra*r*ed *O*bservation *S*atellite), gathered information about weather on the earth; others made it possible to communicate around the globe; and some photographed the earth's surface. What do you think we can learn about the earth from such pictures?

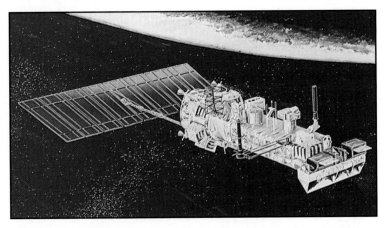

To the Moon

The Soviet Union then sent satellites, the *Lunik* series, to the moon. The first one missed the moon and went on to orbit the sun, just as the planets do. It may continue orbiting, like an artificial planet, for years and years. The second crashed onto the moon, becoming the first manmade object to land on a body in the solar system other than our planet. The third satellite went into orbit around the moon and sent back the first pictures of the dark side of the moon.

The United States sent several *Ranger* probes to the moon to take pictures of its surface. A *probe* is an unmanned spaceship or satellite that has scientific equipment. The spacecraft carried two types of cameras. One type took close-up pictures, and the other took distant pictures. Why do you think that scientists would want to take two kinds of pictures? *Ranger 9,* the last in the series, sent back thousands of excellent photographs right up to the last one-hundredth of a second before it hit the floor of a moon crater.

To Other Planets

The next space satellites went to Venus. Since that planet is covered with heavy clouds, the only way to learn about it was to send a probe to explore it. The United States launched the *Mariner* series to do just that. The probes gathered information as they flew by the planet.

Later probes traveled into the atmosphere of Venus and found that its clouds are made of sulfuric acid. The atmospheric pressure on the planet is almost ninety times the pressure on the earth, and the air has only small amounts of oxygen. Could man live on a planet like this? Most of the probes that traveled through the atmosphere were crushed by the great pressure even before they reached the surface of the planet. Finally, a Russian probe sent back pictures of Venus's surface: it is a dry, hot, barren place.

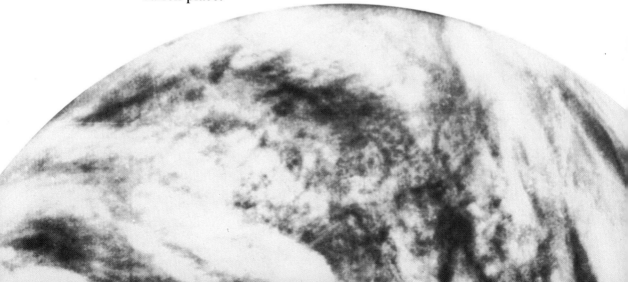

For years science fiction writers and even some
scientists said that life might have "evolved" on Mars.
After sending several spacecraft to orbit the red planet and
to take pictures of its surface, the United States launched
two *Viking* probes to land on the planet. These probes
gave us the first pictures of Mars from the surface. They
also had special arms that gathered samples from the soil
to detect any life that might be present. What do you think
scientists concluded?

The *Pioneer* and *Voyager* probes were the most
ambitious unmanned projects designed by the National
Aeronautics and Space Administration (NASA). *Pioneer
10* and *Pioneer 11* flew by Jupiter in 1972 and 1973.
Pioneer 10 carries a plaque that shows the location of
Earth and has sketches of people on it. Why would
scientists attach a plaque like this to a deep-space probe?
Both probes have since left the solar system. What do you
think will happen to them?

Voyager 2 was launched to fly to Jupiter and beyond to Saturn, Uranus, and Neptune. Scientists discovered some surprising facts about these planets from the reports Voyager sent back to Earth. They saw that one of Jupiter's moons, Io, had volcanoes; they were able to see the detail that God has placed in the rings around Saturn. They found that one of Saturn's moons, Titan, has an atmosphere of methane gas. Methane freezes only at extremely low temperatures; so, although Titan is very cold, scientists have speculated that Titan may have methane rivers and oceans and perhaps even methane rain. With such rain and rivers and oceans, would anything we know of be able to live on Titan?

Voyager then left Saturn and traveled on to Uranus and then to the blue planet, Neptune. The probe showed that Neptune had rings around it, something that was not known before. By the time the tiny craft reached Neptune, it was more than 2.8 billion miles (4.5 billion km) from Earth, and radio signals took more than four hours to travel between controllers on Earth and *Voyager*. How would that delay affect the control of the probe?

It is extremely difficult to steer a vessel toward some other body in space along a path called a *trajectory*. First, everything is moving–the earth, the satellite, and the body that the satellite is aiming for; and all three are moving around the sun. Furthermore, engineers have to allow for the time it takes for radio messages to travel between the vessel and Earth. Seconds can sometimes be crucial. For example, the United States launched *Pioneer 4* to travel within 15,000 miles (24,000 km) of the moon. However, the rocket's engine stayed on one second longer than planned, and the probe flew over 35,000 miles (56,000 km) past its target.

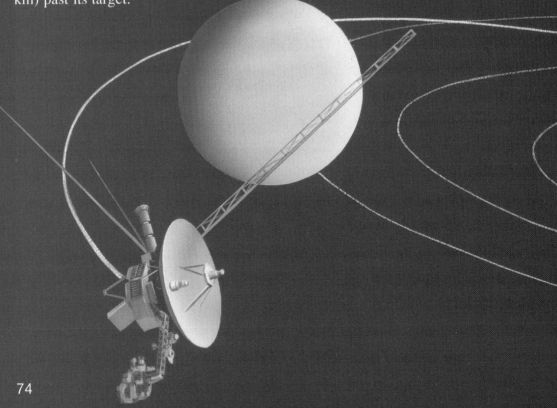

But in 1989, when *Voyager*, almost 3 billion miles (4.8 billion km) from home, went by Neptune, the satellite was a mere 21 miles (34 km) off the course set for it back in 1977 at launching. One scientist said that this accuracy was like making a hole-in-one on a 2,260-mile (3,600-km) golf course. Does this feat mean only that man is brilliant? It clearly demonstrates that the laws God has established in the universe are reliable, and that man's study of mathematics and physics and his explorations must operate within those laws.

Voyager sent back 5 trillion pieces of information during its twelve-year trip through the solar system– enough data to fill 6,000 sets of encyclopedias. Because the probe went out when the planets were all in a line (a pattern that occurs only once every 176 years), it was able to curve around each planet, and using the gravity there, speed up to ''slingshot'' itself toward the next one. This barreling around the planets trimmed twenty years from the 4.5-billion-mile (7.2-billion-km) adventure.

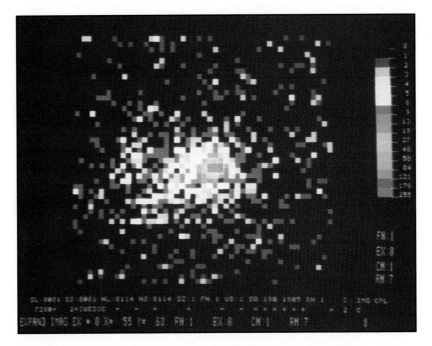

Perhaps you wonder how cameras 2.8 billion miles (4.5 billion km) away can send pictures to Earth. They can hardly mail packages of film back to be processed. Rather, radio waves are the messengers in a technique called *imaging.*

On the *Voyager* is a special 11-millimeter square television screen. When light is reflected onto the screen, its specially coated surface holds the image while a scanner goes over it. The scanner divides the screen into 640,000 spaces called *pixels,* short for "picture elements." If you have ever looked at a newspaper picture under a magnifying glass, you have probably noticed the many dots that make up the picture. Those dots are something like pixels.

The scanner assigns each pixel a number that represents the amount of light in it. A zero means the pixel is completely white. A 256 means the pixel is black. The numbers are then radioed back to Earth where huge dish-shaped antennas pick up the signals. The information is fed into computers that reconstruct the image on television screens here.

Finding Out . . .

About Forces on a Satellite

1. Get a large spool of thread, four or five 1-inch metal washers, 30 inches of string, and your notebook.

2. Put the string through the hole in the spool. Tie one washer to one end and three or four to the other end.

3. Hold the spool over your head, letting the single washer hang down slightly. Holding the spool upright, whirl it in small circles. What happens to the washer? Whirl the spool faster. Now what happens to the washer? What does the single washer represent? What do the string and the other washers represent?

Finding Out . . .

About Imaging

1. Get a clean overhead transparency, your notebook, a black-and-white picture from a newspaper or magazine, black and gray crayons, a transparency pen, and some cellophane tape.

2. Prepare a grid on the transparency with the transparency pen, using the notebook page as a guide. Put the black-and-white picture under the transparency. Line up the upper and left sides of the picture with the upper and left sides of the transparency.

3. Starting with the ''pixel'' in the extreme upper left, decide whether the square is predominantly black, white, or gray. Call out the color you choose to your partner. Let him fill in the corresponding ''pixel'' on his notebook page.

4. Continue across the grid, square by square and row by row, until you have ''transmitted'' all the information from your ''scan'' of the picture. Compare the original with the image. How are they different? How does your decision about the predominant color in each ''pixel'' affect the total image? How could you get a sharper image?

Man in Space

By launching *Sputnik,* man had succeeded in putting a small metal ball into orbit. But putting a man into space would be a much more difficult matter. Can you think of some difficulties that would keep men from going to space? For one thing, the environment of space is harsh indeed. On the earth, God has blessed us with temperatures that we can live in rather easily and has wrapped our world with protective shields of atmosphere. But in space, the temperatures are extreme and there is no protection from the intense radiation of the sun. On the moon, for example, the temperature can rise to 250° F (121° C) and drop to -250° F (157° C). If astronauts were caught in an accident there, they would not be able to survive the environment of space, even for a minute.

Also, when a rocket takes off, it has to overcome the force of gravity. As it begins to travel faster, the astronaut feels as though he weighs much more than he actually does. He is pushed far back into his seat, and he finds it hard to move his body. These forces put much stress on the astronaut.

What kinds of experiments do you think still needed to be done? In 1957, the Soviet Union launched *Sputnik 2.* On board was a dog named Laika. A life-support system was included in the satellite to keep the dog alive, and instruments measured the effects of space travel on the dog. On another trip the Russians sent rats, mice, bugs, plants, and two dogs, and all of them returned to Earth safely. American scientists sent chimpanzees in some of their first capsules to make sure that they were safe for travel.

Preparations

On April 12, 1961, Yuri Gagarin, a Russian, became the first man to travel into space. He orbited the earth once. In May of the same year, Alan B. Shepard became the first American to travel into space; however, he did not travel completely around the earth as Gagarin did. That honor went to John Glenn in 1962. All the exploration programs up to this time were steps toward the most adventurous goal of all: to send a man to the moon.

Before men visited the moon, they needed to study its surface, gravity, and soil. Why? What risks would men be taking by trying to land on the moon without this information? What else would astronauts need in order to make a successful landing? For one thing, they would need a good map. How do you think they could get a map of the moon? From the pictures earlier spacecraft had sent back, scientists were able to make the necessary detailed maps.

The men in space would also need a special suit to protect them from all the dangers: the lack of air, the heat, the cold, the radiations, and tiny meteors called *micrometeoroids,* nearly invisible bits of matter moving at 64,000 miles (103,000 km) an hour.

The astronaut's space suit is made up of three suits. It contains everything needed for the astronaut's survival in space. What do you think the suit provides for the astronaut? The innermost suit, the *union suit,* is made of a number of tubes that are embedded in a fabric with spaces in it. The tubes are attached to the backpack, a *portable life-support system,* where water and oxygen are stored.

The middle layer is the *diver's suit,* the pressure garment. Made of rubber and different fabrics, it maintains the atmospheric pressure necessary for human life and protects against oxygen leakage. This part is also linked to the life-support system, where contaminants such as carbon dioxide are removed.

The outer part of the suit is a type of armor to guard the pressure suit underneath. Made of thirteen layers, this outer part protects the astronaut from ultraviolet rays and other radiation as well as from micrometeoroids. Even though it is a hard, protective suit–it feels like an inflated football–it allows the astronaut to move rather easily. It also has a compressed food bar inside the helmet and a tube for sipping a drink from a bag in the neck ring of the suit. In the astronaut's backpack is a communication system that lets him talk with the other astronauts or ground control.

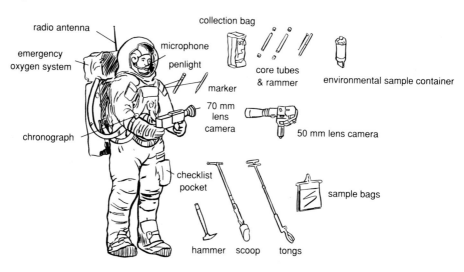

To the Moon

Apollo 11, 300 feet (91.44 m) tall and weighing over 3,000 tons (2,900 metric tons), made space-flight history. What stages do you see in the rocket? Can you describe its course to the moon?

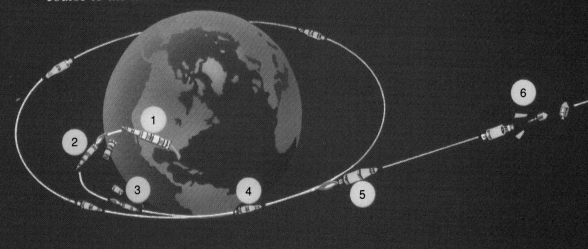

1. Liftoff
2. First stage separates; second stage fires (41 miles [66 km] up)
3. Second stage separates; third stage fires (116 miles [187 km] up)
4. Spacecraft enters "parking orbit"
5. Third stage refires; *Apollo 11* heads for the moon
6. Third stage separates from craft; craft docks with lunar module

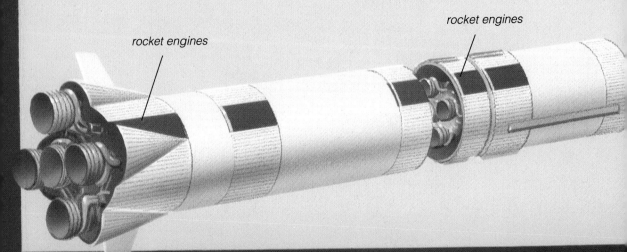

rocket engines

rocket engines

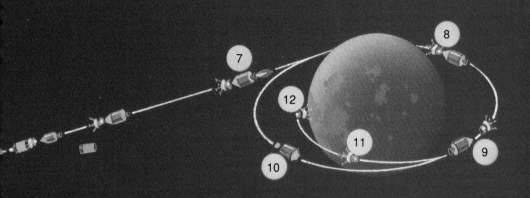

7. Service module fires into orbit around moon
8. Two astronauts transfer to lunar module
9. Lunar module separates
10. Command and service modules go into "parking orbit"
11. Lunar module descends
12. Lunar module lands on moon

propulsion engine

Service Module (contained the rocket engines and fuel to correct course)

Command Module (contained controls, radio equipment, fuel, food, and parachutes)

rocket engine

launch escape system

Lunar Module (the part that landed on the moon; had two stages–one for landing and one for lifting off)

# ACTION

Astronautics

Astro comes from a word meaning "star," and *naut* comes from words meaning "sailor" or "ship." What is the literal meaning of the word *astronaut?* It means "sailor among the stars." *Astronautics* is the study of what traveling among the stars requires.

What do you think the men were like who were first chosen to go to the moon? They were carefully selected by the National Aeronautics and Space Administration (NASA), based on several standards. Each astronaut had to be a citizen of the United States (or plan to become one), be either a scientist or a pilot, have many years of classroom training, be under six feet tall, be under forty years old, and be in good physical condition. The pilots also had to have logged hundreds of hours of flying time.

Neil Armstrong, the *Apollo 11* mission commander, took his first airplane ride at age six and had earned his pilot's license by his sixteenth birthday. He flew seventy-eight combat missions in the Korean War. He earned a degree in aeronautical engineering from Purdue University, and he had been on the *Gemini 8* mission in 1966.

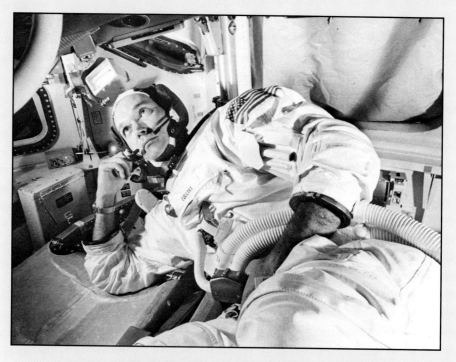

The command module commander, Michael Collins, was a West Point graduate and an Air Force test pilot. He had been on the *Gemini 10* and had walked in space twice. Edwin Aldrin commanded the lunar module. Graduated from West Point and holding a doctorate from Massachusetts Institute of Technology, "Buzz" was considered the "best scientific mind in space"–he could catch a computer in a mistake. He had been an Air Force pilot and had been on the *Gemini 12* mission, walking in space in 1966. What qualifications did all three men have in common?

Once they were selected, the astronauts spent from a year to two and a half years getting more training. They took more classes in astronomy, physics, geology, anatomy, and computer science. They worked in computer-controlled *simulators,* specially built rooms that provided conditions they would have in outer space. They practiced eating, drinking, and moving in weightlessness. And they trained to stay alive after their spacecraft returned to Earth, learning how to get out of the ship and how to land in emergency situations.

Landing on the Moon

The astronauts in the lunar module (nicknamed *Eagle*) were to land in the Sea of Tranquility, a rocky plain on the moon. Automatic controls slowly lowered the *Eagle* to within a few thousand feet of the moon's surface. Armstrong and Aldrin strained to see the surface to check the landing spot. Suddenly, Armstrong saw that the *Eagle* was heading instead for a rocky crater. He decided to take over manual control, to try to guide the *Eagle* past the crater. Communication blacked out between the earth and the *Eagle*. The fuel light flashed on, warning that fuel was running low. Armstrong held the *Eagle* skimming, hovering over the surface. Forty-five seconds left . . . thirty seconds. . . . Still Armstrong kept the craft above the surface, looking for a place to put down. Then, with only twenty seconds to spare, he calmly rocked the hand controller, and the *Eagle* softly landed. Almost immediately came Aldrin's voice, "O.K., engine stop." Just seconds later Armstrong announced to Houston: "Tranquility Base here. The *Eagle* has landed." A voice from Houston replied: "Roger, Tranquility, we copy you on the ground. You got a bunch of guys about to turn blue. We're breathing again. Thanks a lot." The time was 4:17 P.M., July 20, 1969.

Eight days after the towering 3,200-ton *Apollo 11* lifted off, the three astronauts were plowing back through Earth's atmosphere at 25,000 miles (40,000 km) an hour in a small cone, all that was left of the many stages. At 23,000 feet (7 km) above the Pacific Ocean, three huge parachutes whipped open, and minutes later man's first trip to the moon ended with a splash south of Hawaii.

The rock and soil samples that Armstrong and Aldrin had collected and even the astronauts themselves were put into isolation for more than two weeks. Why do you think this precaution was taken? Later scientists from all over the United States and from a few other countries studied the moon rocks and the dust and the soil. What do you think they looked for?

INSIDE Information

Inside a special lunar container were about 45 pounds (20 kg) of moon rocks. They were mostly cocoa and gray-colored, covered with dust that–at first–was thought to be potentially dangerous. Most of the rocks were *igneous*, formed by heat. What might be one explanation for that? The rocks also contained three times as much of the element titanium as is found in the earth's crust, and an abundance of tiny glassy beads. How would this data change the theory that the moon was once a part of the earth? All the rocks were measured, photographed, labeled, and analyzed. Some moon rocks have been on public display. Have you ever seen one?

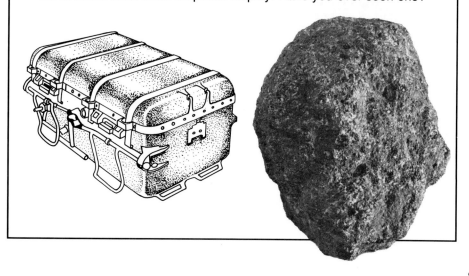

Since 1969, ten more astronauts have walked on the moon. And space shuttles have taken satellites into space and retrieved malfunctioning ones. Man looks at his mighty achievements with pride, planning for space travel in the future that is not very different from what is now only science fiction.

Yet man has, with immense effort and cost, gone only to the moon, a tiny satellite around the third planet of an obscure solar system in a galaxy that is but one in hundreds of billions of galaxies. Our best accomplishments fade to nothing beside the immeasurable span of God's creation. The best result of the space program is to reveal, if only in a small way, some of the glory of God.

"If I ascend up into heaven, thou art there."
Psalm 139:8

Respiratory System

"And the Lord God formed man of the dust of the ground, and breathed into his nostrils the breath of life; and man became a living soul."   *Genesis 2:7*

Every day you operate one of the most efficient and complex air purification systems in the world, and most of the time you do not even think about it. This system processes more than 2,640 gallons (10,000 liters) of air every twenty-four hours, more than 924,000 gallons (3.5 million liters) a year. This system is automatic and fully portable. It requires little maintenance. It can function in any climate. What do you think such machinery might be worth? It is priceless. And it is but one of the many treasures God has given you in your body.

Parts of the Respiratory System

Another name for breathing is *respiration,* from two word parts meaning "to breathe again." Why do we have to breathe again and again our whole lives through? What happens to the air that we draw in? How does this process help us live?

When you think about breathing, you probably think about your nose and your lungs and perhaps your mouth. But many more structures are involved in bringing oxygen into your body. Breathing does not even really start with your nose; but it is easier to follow the path of air from the outside to the inside of your body.

When you breathe in, air passes through your nose or mouth into the back of your throat. If you breathe through your nose, air is filtered by many tiny hairs and special membranes that produce *mucus,* a thick, sticky substance. Mucus also warms and moistens the air. Why do you think it is better for your body to receive warm, moist air than cold, dry air?

The air goes from the nose or mouth to the throat. The throat branches into a windpipe, called the *trachea,* and a food pipe, called the *esophagus.* Where they meet is a kind of traffic director, called the *epiglottis,* a thin flap of tissue. When you swallow, the epiglottis bends and shuts down on the windpipe like a lid. What do you think happens when the epiglottis does not completely close? Sometimes food or liquid gets into the windpipe. And then what happens? You cough. Your body tries to get the food or drink out before it goes any farther into your respiratory system.

The trachea branches again into two open tubes which lead to the *lungs,* fleshy bags where the real business of breathing is done. In the lungs the tubes branch many times into smaller and smaller tubes, each finally ending in clusters of tiny sacs. You might picture the lungs with all the branching tubes as a many-limbed tree with berries at the end of every twig.

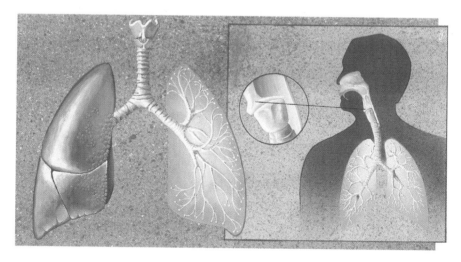

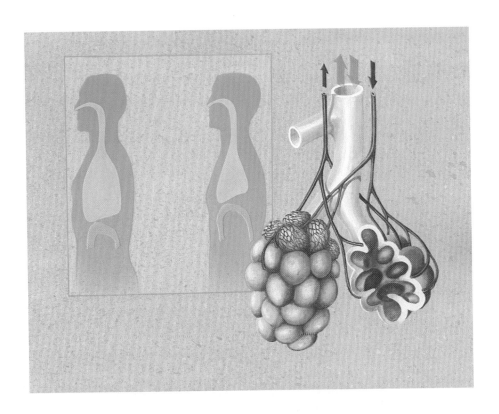

Air passes through the trachea and travels through the branching tubes until it comes into the tiny sacs. Although each sac is extremely small—you may have around 600 million in your lungs—they would cover a tennis court if they were all flattened out. All around the air sacs are tiny blood vessels with walls only one cell thick. Gases from the air you have breathed in pass easily from the sacs into the vessels, getting into your blood.

Air could not come into your body at all if it were not for one important muscle called the *diaphragm*. This strong sheet of muscle—shaped like an upside-down saucer—is attached to the lower ribs and the backbone. It separates your chest from your abdomen horizontally. When the diaphragm tightens, it pulls down. Does that movement increase or decrease the amount of space in the chest? It increases it. What do you think happens to the lungs? What do you think happens when the muscle relaxes? What happens to the lungs?

Finding Out . . .

About Breathing

1. Get a glass lamp chimney, two large balloons, some modeling clay, a plastic straw or rubber tubing, and a thick rubber band.

2. Slit one balloon and spread it over the bottom opening of the chimney. Secure it with the rubber band. Fit the other balloon over the straw or tubing. Then, holding the balloon in the lamp chimney, put modeling clay around the straw, closing the upper opening completely. Be sure the balloon hangs in the center of the chimney.

3. Hold the chimney around the narrow part. Gently pull down on the balloon stretched across the bottom. What happens to the balloon inside the chimney? Let go of the stretched balloon. Now what happens to the balloon inside the chimney? Push in on the stretched balloon. What happens? How do you think that your diaphragm functions? What does the muscle have to do for you to breathe in? Complete the diagram on your notebook page.

Why Do We Breathe?

When the diaphragm pulls tight, air rushes into the respiratory system, traveling the path you have already read about. You can hold your breath for a little while, but your body will force you to take another breath eventually. God has designed your respiratory system to keep bringing in the life-giving air. Have you ever wondered why air is so important to life? It is something like the fuel in a car–our bodies need air to generate energy.

What is in that air? Mostly gases such as oxygen, nitrogen, and carbon dioxide. The oxygen in air is what we need most. When oxygen passes into the blood from the air sacs, it is carried throughout the body. It combines with digested food to make energy and heat. Just as a fire needs air to burn, so your body needs air to use the energy from food.

The release of energy produces carbon dioxide. Since your body cannot use much carbon dioxide, it gets rid of most of it by breathing out. You can never squeeze all the air out of your lungs though. Even if you try your hardest to blow it all out, there will still be more than a quart left inside–that would fill more than four of the cartons you get milk in at lunch. It is something like squeezing an accordion closed; some air must remain or the accordion would collapse.

Your brain controls how fast and how deeply you breathe. Certain receptors in your body are always testing the blood that passes through, checking the carbon dioxide level. When your brain registers that there is too much carbon dioxide in the blood, it signals your system to take in fresh air and send out the old.

Do you use more energy when you sit or when you run? When you sleep or when you jump rope? When you read or when you bounce a basketball? Whenever you are moving, you use more energy. And when you need more energy, you need more oxygen to mix with your fuel–the food you have digested. Your brain tells your lungs to work harder and faster when you exercise. It regulates just how fast and deeply you should breathe for the work you are doing.

What do you think happens when you breathe more heavily than your body needs? You sometimes get light-headed; you may even faint. What do you think would make someone breathe abnormally fast or deep? Usually some emotion like fear or anger. Such emotions have many unpleasant and harmful results in our bodies. No wonder the Bible has so much to say about controlling emotions. God has carefully designed our brains to measure precisely our breathing needs and has advised us how best to live with that wonderful design.

How Much Air Do Lungs Hold?

The amount of air that can be taken into the lungs is called *lung capacity*. A normal breath takes in about a pint of air, enough to fill two small milk cartons. Breathing normally, we use only about one-eighth of the space in our lungs. How many cartons do you think a big breath would fill? Can you tell why your chest does not get eight times bigger when you take a deep breath? The tiny air sacs make efficient use of space.

A person usually breathes about twelve times a minute. How much air goes into the lungs in a minute at that rate? Twelve pints. But during exercise the brain may signal that the the body needs more than seventeen times that much air. About how much would that be? If a deep breath pulls in eight pints, how many times a minute would you have to breathe deeply to meet the need?

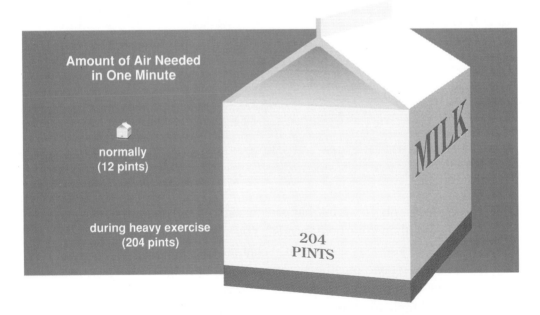

Amount of Air Needed
in One Minute

normally
(12 pints)

during heavy exercise
(204 pints)

204
PINTS

MILK

By the time a man is about seventy years old, he will have breathed in enough air to fill a large oil tanker. Do you think a professional athlete would be able to fill a larger tanker?

Finding Out . . .

About Lung Capacity

1. Get a glass jar, a large glass dish, a rubber tube or a bendable straw, four bolts, some water, some masking tape, a measuring cup or cylinder, and a pen.

2. Put a strip of masking tape straight down the side of the jar. Then set up the remaining equipment as you did for the *Finding Out About Gases Exchanged in Breathing*. Be sure that the jar is full of water or that you mark the top of the water on the tape when the jar is still upright.

3. Take a normal breath and blow it into the straw. Mark the new water level. Remove the jar as you did in the other activity. Fill the jar with water again or fill it to the mark you made before you set up the equipment. Pour out water into the measuring cup or cylinder until the water level drops to the line you made after breathing into the straw. How much water is in the cup or cylinder? How much air did you breathe out? Record your findings.

4. Set up the equipment again. This time take as deep a breath as you can and blow into the straw all the air you can. Mark the new water level. Measure the amount of air as you did before. How do the two measurements compare?

97

Finding Out . . .

About Gases Exchanged
in Breathing

1. Get two narrow-mouthed pint jars, a rubber tube or a bendable straw, a large glass bowl, two candles, matches, some water, a piece of stiff plastic, and four large bolts.

2. Fill the bowl and one of the jars with water. Place the stiff plastic over the mouth of the jar and turn the jar upside-down in the bowl of water. Pull out the piece of plastic. Then place the bolts under the jar so that it is raised evenly off the bottom of the bowl. (If you are working with a partner, one of you may just want to hold the lip of the jar below the water.) Slip one end of the rubber tube or straw into the jar.

3. Blow through the tube or straw until all the water in the jar has been replaced with exhaled air. Breathe out naturally; do not blow forcibly. Keeping the lip of the jar under the water, raise the jar and slip the plastic under it. Put the jar upside-down on the table.

4. Light both candles. Quickly, and at the same time, put the jar of exhaled air over one candle and a jar of ordinary air over the other.

5. Which candle goes out first? Can you explain why?

Finding Out . . .

How Exercise Affects Breathing

1. Get your science partner, a stopwatch or a clock with a second hand, and your notebook.

2. Count the number of times your partner breathes in one minute. Record the number. Let him count the number of times you breathe in a minute. He should record the number. (If you want, you can multiply the amount of air you breathed out in a normal breath in *Finding Out About Lung Capacity* by the number of breaths you take in a minute to find how much air you need per minute.)

3. Have your partner do thirty jumping jacks. Immediately count how many times he breathes in one minute. Record the number. Then you do thirty jumping jacks. Let your partner count how many times you breathe in one minute.

4. When your breathing rate returns to normal, try other activities or exercises. What has the most influence on your breathing?

Clearing the Airways

The tiny hairs that line your nose are your first defense against dirt in the air. The trachea and all the other tubes in your respiratory system also have little hairlike structures called *cilia*. In the lungs, in all the branches there, cilia move constantly. You might picture their movement as looking something like wheat fields when wind blows over them or the bristles of a hairbrush when you run your thumb across them.

Their wavelike motion moves the mucus and the dirt it has trapped out of the lungs. When the mucus reaches the throat–coming from either the nose or the lungs–it goes to the stomach in a swallow and is no longer a threat to your health.

INSIDE Information

Sometimes, when you have a cold or are working in a dusty place, the respiratory system needs more than the action of cilia to keep the air passages clean. A cough blasts out of the lungs at nearly 360 miles (580 km) an hour. When you cough, your diaphragm pulls tight suddenly, air pressure builds up, and air is violently released through your mouth. A sneeze happens in much the same way, except the air rushes out through your nose. Some sneezes shoot air out at jet speed–faster than sound.

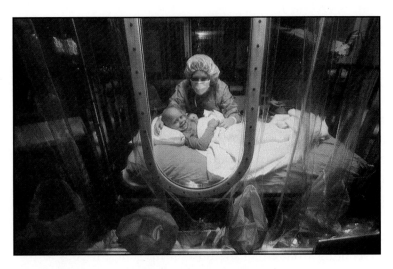

Problems with Breathing

Asthma is a disorder that causes the small tubes in the lungs to become narrow from time to time. People with asthma often use special devices to help them breathe better. *Bronchitis* is a problem caused when the tubes swell. The mucus then partly blocks the airways and makes it hard to breathe.

Some people cannot breathe in as much dust or pollen as other people. Their bodies respond greatly to material in the air that many others never notice. These people often sneeze, have runny noses, and suffer with itchy eyes. Their reaction is called an *allergy*. One of the most common allergies is *hay fever,* although it is not caused only by hay. Many kinds of pollen bring it on. What time of year do you think hay fever happens most?

The respiratory problem almost everyone reading this book has had is a cold, an infection of the respiratory system. No one has found a cure for this disorder. The best you can do is stay warm, drink a lot of water and fruit juices, and rest. God has equipped your body to deal with such illnesses. Your system steps up mucus production to trap foreign material; you cough and sneeze; you even get a fever which helps kill the virus that is making you sick.

You can help your respiratory system avoid some problems. Cold and flu viruses float around in the air all the time. They get into your system through your nose and mouth. The defenses there can normally handle the usual amount of germs coming in. But when you add to the burden by eating without washing your hands or putting your fingers or pencils in your mouth, you increase the chances of catching a cold.

A healthy lung is pinkish. A smoker's lungs are gray and black. What causes the difference? Cigarette smoke damages cilia. Often the cilia stop moving altogether. What do you think happens then? Dust, germs, and dirt from the smoke stay in the lungs. Why do you think smokers and people who breathe other people's smoke have worse colds and more lung diseases than people who breathe clean air? Their best defenses have been paralyzed. After a while, smokers get serious diseases like lung cancer. They also get cancer of the throat, the stomach, and the kidneys.

I Corinthians 6:19-20 tells us that our bodies are the temple of the living God. We are the caretakers; we should not do anything that would harm our health. To take proper care of our bodies is to obey the Lord who made them and lent them to us.

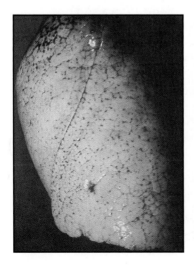 

What Breathing Has To Do with Talking

At the top of your trachea in the front of your throat is a small hollow ring of tough fiber. Two leathery bands– *vocal folds*–stretch over this ring, and there is a small gap shaped like a triangle between them. Together these parts make up your voice box, or *larynx*. You may have heard someone call it his "Adam's apple." Without this amazing equipment, you could not speak.

Every breath you take passes through the larynx, through the space between the vocal folds. When the folds are relaxed, air rushes through quietly. When the vocal folds are pulled closer together, they vibrate as the air goes by. The vibration is sound. The tighter the folds are stretched, the higher the sound they will make. The process is a little like stretching the neck of a balloon as air escapes. If you pull the balloon tight, there is a squeal; if you let the neck go, the air comes out in a much lower sound.

To form words or sing songs from these vibrations takes many other parts–the tongue, the lips, the teeth, the jaw, the cheeks, and more. God has not only given us the special equipment we need for speaking, He has also shown us the true purpose for using them: to praise Him. When we speak, we should honor Him who made it possible for us to speak. And when it occurs to you that you are taking in life-giving air, it should cause you to remember, as Daniel said, "the God in whose hand thy breath is."

"The spirit of God hath made me, and the breath of the Almighty hath given me life."

Job 33:4

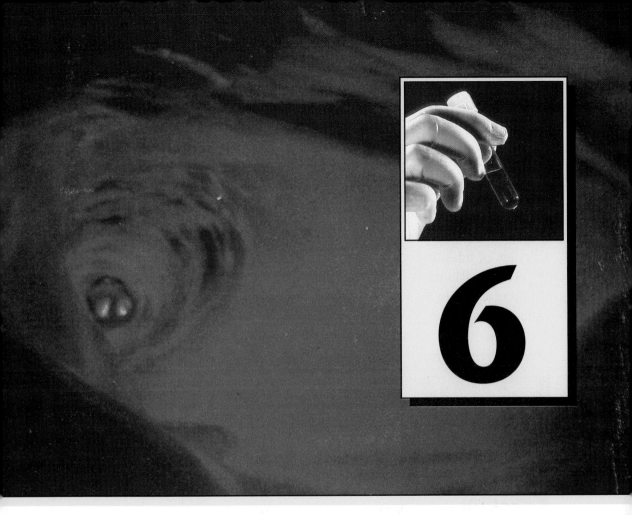

 # Circulation

"The life of the flesh is in the blood."

Leviticus 17:11

When you look at the back of your hand or the underside of your wrist, you can see blood vessels under your skin. Your body is packed with these vessels, some as thick as a garden hose and some thinner than a thread. Every cell in your body–except a few in your eyes–gets fuel and oxygen from one of these vessels. There are trillions of cells in your body. To nourish them all requires a system of tubes incredibly complicated and long. If all the vessels in an adult's body were laid end to end, they would reach more than 60,000 miles (96,000 km), almost enough to go around the earth two and a half times.

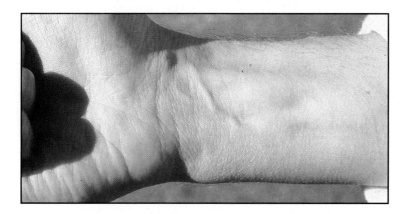

Through this network of vessels flows a liquid that contains, among other materials, oxygen, germ-fighters, clot-makers, and nutrients from food digested earlier. It is a liquid that you cannot do without, not even for a minute–your blood. An adult has about 10 to 12 pints (5 to 6 liters) of blood. You have somewhat less, depending on your size. How do you think so much blood is kept moving through 60,000 miles (96,000 km) of vessels, making a complete trip every twenty seconds, every day as long as you live? God has designed the perfect machinery for the task, and no invention of man has even come close to copying it.

Parts of the Circulatory System

The Heart

The great force that keeps the blood moving is the *heart,* the pump of life. It pumps out about 3 tablespoon-fuls every eight-tenths of a second, or 5 quarts a minute, which adds up to about 10 tons a day. It does enough work in one hour to lift 1.5 tons a foot off the ground. How much work does it do by the end of each day?

It seems likely that this powerful pump would be rather heavy and large. But a man's heart is about the size of his fist and weighs just about as much as a can of soda that you get from a vending machine. A woman's heart usually weighs less than a man's, about 9 ounces.

The heart is strong because it is almost all muscle. It is held in a slippery sac so that when it pumps it does not rub directly against the lungs or the wall of the chest. Why is it important that the heart not rub against the lungs? The rubbing could keep the heart from working as efficiently. The sac functions something like oil on a bicycle chain.

The heart actually works like two pumps together, one pumping blood to the lungs and one pumping blood to the body. Blood that has given oxygen to cells in your body comes back to the right side of your heart. That side pushes the blood to your lungs where it picks up more oxygen. Then the other side of the heart receives the blood from the lungs and pumps it out to the body. Blood coming into the heart is a purplish blue; the blood returning from the lungs and going out to the body again is bright red. What do you think causes the change?

INSIDE Information

God has designed the heart to pump precisely. The right side pumps gently, sending just enough blood to the lungs to gather oxygen. The left side pumps with four times as much force, forcing the blood out on its many-mile trip through the body. Yet both sides pump at the same time, making blood flow evenly and constantly.

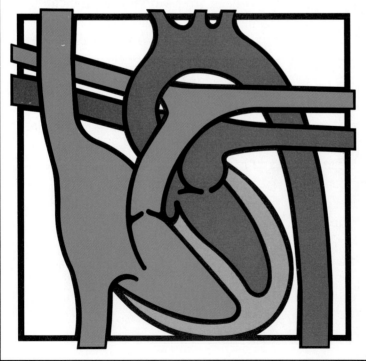

In the heart the blood without oxygen does not normally mix with the blood carrying oxygen. The heart has specially designed safeguards against that. First, the two pumping parts of the heart are separated by a wall of special tissue. Second, the heart and blood vessels have *valves*, small gates that swing only one way. Blood can go through, but it cannot flow back. If you listen to someone's heartbeat, you hear two sounds in each beat, rather like "lub-dub." Those are the sounds of valves in the heart slapping shut.

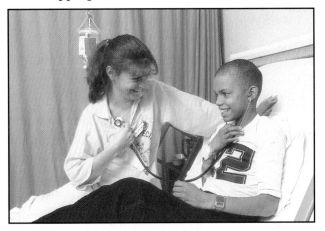

Doctors can tell much about how the heart is functioning by listening to the sounds it makes. Years ago a doctor simply put his ear to the patient's chest and listened. But when one doctor had a patient so heavy that he could not hear the heart clearly, he rolled some stiff paper into a tube and held it to the patient's chest. Then he could hear the heartbeats. Today's doctors use much better devices, called *stethoscopes*, but they work on the same principle.

Doctors can sometimes replace damaged heart valves with manmade ones. The new valves wear out in a few years under the constant opening and closing. The valves of a normal heart, however, open and close more than 250 million times in seventy-five years, precisely, continuously, without repair, without a single thought from the owner.

How the Heart Sounds

1. Get $2\frac{1}{4}$ feet of rubber tubing, a T-tube or a Y-tube, and three small glass funnels.

2. Cut a piece of tubing 3 inches long. Cut two pieces of tubing a foot long. Put one end of the 3-inch tubing over the tip of the funnel. Push the T-tube (or Y-tube) into the other end. Slip the longer pieces of tubing over each arm of the T-tube. Put funnels in each end of the longer tubes.

3. Hold the wide end of the funnel firmly over your heart. Let your science partner put the other two funnels over his ears. He must press the funnels against his ears firmly to exclude outside noise. Let him describe what he hears. Then do fifteen jumping jacks. Let him listen again. What do you think he hears now? Hold the funnel for him so that he can hear his own heart. After he listens, trade positions. What do you hear? Describe what you hear. Can you explain what causes the louder sound you hear? What changes do you hear after the jumping jacks? Listen to your own heart. Does it sound different from your partner's?

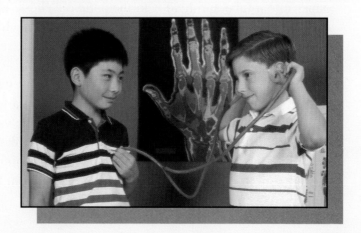

The heart has its own motor, a little cluster of cells that sends out an electric current to the heart muscle, making the heart *contract,* or squeeze up. These cells send out the signal to contract about eighty or ninety times a minute in young people and around seventy times a minute in adults. More than 100,000 times a day your pacemaker cells spark your heart to action. Perhaps you know someone who has had a manmade pacemaker put in his heart. What do you think the device does?

The only rest your heart gets is between beats. When you are sitting still, your heart may beat ten fewer times in a minute. When you are sleeping, it may beat twenty fewer times. Why do you think it is important to get enough sleep? If one heartbeat produces 2 foot-pounds of energy, how much work do you save your heart by going to bed an hour early? Exercising your heart is important, too. The stronger your heart is, the fewer times it must beat per minute. How does having a strong heartbeat help your heart get rest?

The number of times your heart beats in a certain length of time is called your *heart rate.* You can figure your heart rate by counting the times you can feel your *pulse,* or the little jump in your blood vessels following your heart beats. You can feel (and sometimes even see) your pulse on several places on your body. The easiest place to take your pulse is probably on your wrist.

Finding Out . . .

About Heart Rate

1. Get a stopwatch or a watch with a second hand, some weights or heavy books, and your notebook.

2. Place your right index and middle fingers on the underside of your left wrist. Can you feel the pulse? After you have been sitting still for a few minutes, count how many pulses you feel in fifteen seconds. Record that number and multiply it by four. Record the number.

3. Now stand and walk at a normal pace around the room for at least two minutes. Take your pulse for fifteen seconds. Record it and multiply by four. How does it compare with the pulse you took earlier. Is there a difference? Can you explain the difference?

4. Sit quietly until your pulse rate returns to the level you recorded at the beginning. Then stand, take the weights or books in your arms, and walk at the same speed as before for two minutes. Take your pulse for fifteen seconds. Record the number and multiply by four. What does the pulse rate show? What effect do you think being overweight has on your heart?

5. Let your heart rate return to normal. Then, making sure that you are at least arm's length from everyone else, do jumping jacks for one minute. Take your pulse as you did before. Record all your readings.

The Blood Vessels

The major blood vessels are classified by the direction in which they carry blood. The vessels carrying blood toward the heart are *veins;* vessels carrying blood away from the heart are *arteries.* Which vessels are carrying red blood? Why do you think that no matter where you get cut, the blood that you see is red? What do you think happens to oxygen-low blood that is exposed to air?

Blood is forced out of the heart into a large artery, which branches into smaller vessels. Those vessels branch millions of times more, until some blood is passing into blood vessels smaller around than a hair. These smallest vessels in the body are the *capillaries.* The walls of capillaries are so thin that oxygen and nutrients can pass right through them to the cells they touch.

It is in these tiny tubes that blood, its oxygen released, starts back toward the heart. The purplish blue blood travels through the capillaries, emptying into larger and larger veins until it reaches the right side of the heart. What happens to the blood then?

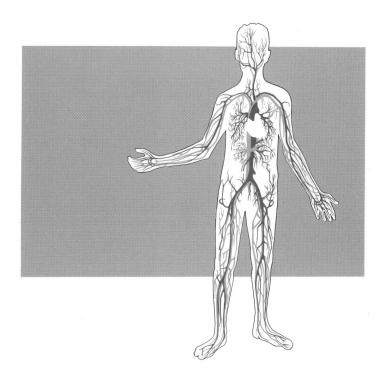

The Blood

Blood is made of *plasma,* a yellow liquid about the consistency of gelatin before it sets, and several kinds of cells. When plasma is separated from the cells, you can see that the cells account for slightly more than half of the blood.

One kind of blood cell is the *red cell.* Can you tell by their color what the main job of these cells is? They carry oxygen. There are countless millions of red cells in your blood. In fact, several million of them would fit in the period at the end of this sentence.

The red cells look somewhat like tiny rubber rafts or miniscule throat lozenges, round and concave on top and bottom. Small as they are, red cells often have to twist to get through capillaries that are only one cell wide. Mostly they are pushed through by red cells piling up behind them. Despite the sometimes rough travel, a red cell can make about 160,000 trips through the heart before it wears out and dies.

Red cells are made in the center of your bones, in a tissue called *marrow.* If you have ever seen a chicken bone broken open or the center of the cut bone in a piece of ham, you have probably seen some bone marrow. Your marrow produces more than a million new red cells every second. They move into your bloodstream and begin moving toward your lungs to do the work of picking up oxygen.

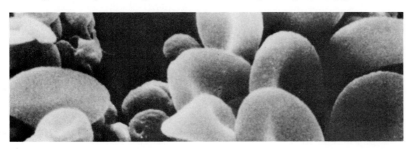

Another kind of cell in the blood is the *white cell.* White cells are bigger than red cells–only a few thousand white cells would fit into the period at the end of this sentence–and there are fewer of them. The main job of white cells is to scout out invading germs and to destroy them. Many times a white cell ''swallows'' an invader and traps or digests it. At other times, the white cell detects a *toxin,* or poison, in the invader. Then it produces an *antitoxin,* a substance that makes the toxin harmless. Why does the white cell not swallow toxin-producers?

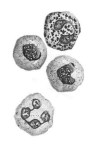

Platelets are cell fragments that protect your body from germs in another, less direct way. When you cut yourself and bleed, the platelets release a clotting substance that, together with other materials from the blood vessel and the blood, form a plug that will slow down the loss of blood. If the cut is not severe, the clot will stop the bleeding soon and harden into a scab. Can you think of two reasons you should not pick a scab loose? You may open the cut and cause bleeding again, and you will remove the barrier your body has made for holding out germs until the skin grows back.

Cardiology

The study of the heart is called *cardiology,* from the Greek words *kardia* (heart) and *logia* (science or study). A person who studies the heart and tries to mend damaged ones is a *cardiologist.* It takes at least eight years of medical school to become a cardiologist. Can you think of some reasons for so much training?

Doctors have been trying many methods for helping heart patients. They have added manmade vessels to the heart, taken vessels from the leg and patched heart vessels, put in artificial hearts, substituted baboon hearts for human hearts, and even transplanted a heart from one person to another. Some of these techniques have helped to prevent serious heart problems or to correct some of the damage of heart disease. Replacing clogged vessels with vessels from the leg, for example, can add many healthy years to a person's life.

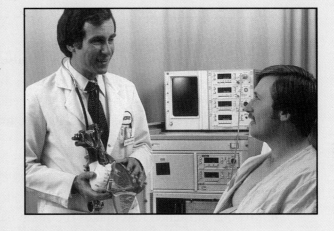

Other methods, such as using an artificial heart, are not much more than experiments right now. The finest manmade heart still cannot do what the physical heart can do. Without the intricate connections with the nervous system, the mechanical heart cannot respond as efficiently and quickly as a real heart.

Cardiologists are constantly researching to discover how they can better work with the masterful, complex design of the human body to help keep the all-important pump in operation.

Blood Types

About five hundred years ago, the Inca Indians were saving people's lives by putting blood from one person into the blood vessels of another person, using a tube. But when, many years later, doctors in other countries tried to transfer blood this way, most patients got worse instead of better. It was not until recently that scientists began to understand that there are different kinds of blood–four main kinds, in fact–and that some kinds cannot mix with the others.

The blood types are labeled *O, A, B,* and *AB.* The labels tell what kind of special substances are in the blood. Some people have only the *A* substance; some have only the *B;* some have both; some have neither. When type *A* blood receives type *B* blood, cells called *antibodies* in the *A* blood read the *B* substances as enemies. In trying to get rid of the enemy, the antibodies cause the *B* substances to clump together, clogging blood vessels. Today when doctors transfer blood, or give *transfusions,* they make sure the types are compatible.

One type can mix with all the other kinds with no bad results. Which kind do you think that is? Type *O,* because it has neither *A* nor *B* substances, can safely mix with any other kind of blood. Which type do you think can receive all the other types? Type *AB* can. Do you think *AB* can ever be given to any of the others? Why?

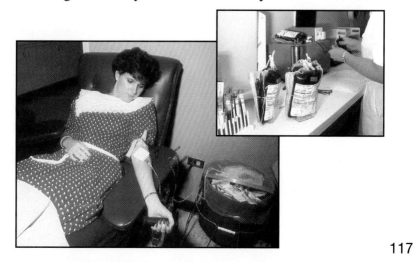

Finding Out . . .

About Blood Types

1. Get four clear glasses or test tubes, some water, red and blue food coloring, four blank note cards, a pen, and your notebook.

2. Fill each glass half full of water. Add to the first glass enough red food coloring to make the water a rich red. Add to the second glass enough blue coloring to make the water a rich blue. To the third glass add red and blue to make a definite purple. Leave the fourth glass colorless.

3. Using a note card, label the red glass *Type A*. Label the blue glass *Type B,* and the purple glass *Type AB*. Label the colorless water *Type O*.

4. Predict which glasses can be poured into others without changing the color. (Colors can be lightened or darkened, but not changed to another color.)

5. Pour water from glass to glass according to your predictions. Record what happens. Were your predictions correct?

6. Fill in the chart, showing what blood types can be transfused to other types.

BLOOD PRESSURE

120/80   130/80   150/80   200/80

Blood Pressure

Perhaps you have heard someone say he was going to have his blood pressure taken. What does that mean? It means he is going to measure how much "push" the blood in his arteries has. The measurement is always a fraction, such as $\frac{120}{80}$. The numbers show how much pressure the blood is causing on the walls of arteries.

A special machine called a *sphygmomanometer* (sfig′mō•mə•nom′i•tər) measures blood pressure. It tells how high the force of your pumping blood can push mercury in a glass tube. If you have ever seen someone at a circus or a fair trying to make a bell ring by hitting a lever with a mallet, you have some idea of how a sphygmomanometer works. Some sphygmomanometers have dials instead of mercury columns, but they operate on the same principle.

120

When a doctor takes someone's blood pressure, he wraps a band of material around the person's upper arm. He pumps air into the band until the cuff temporarily shuts blood flow in an artery. Then he puts his stethoscope on the artery and lets air slowly out of the band. When blood begins to flow again, it makes a sound that the doctor can hear in the stethoscope. At that exact moment, he reads the height of the mercury in the tube. That reading is the top number in the fraction. When he can no longer hear the sound, when the heart is at rest, he reads the mercury again, and that reading becomes the bottom number in the fraction.

Which number in the fraction do you think shows the maximum push in the artery? What do you think a reading of $\frac{200}{90}$ means? It means that either the heart is pumping too hard or that the arteries are too narrow for some reason for the amount of blood that is coming through. The condition is called high blood pressure. It is dangerous, sometimes even deadly.

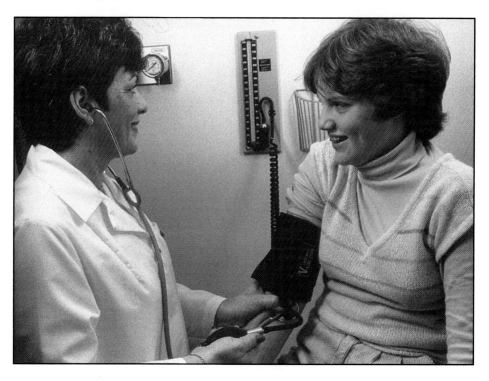

No one is sure what causes high blood pressure. Lately, doctors have come to understand what the Bible has always said: strong emotions affect your health. Anger, fear, greed, and hate can drive the blood pressure up. Contentedness, love, and unselfishness can bring the blood pressure down. When you talk, your blood pressure goes up; when you listen, it goes down. When you worry, it shoots up; when you pray, it drops to levels that usually come only after many hours of sleep. By following the guidelines God has given us in His word, we not only learn how to be better Christians, but we also find ourselves in better health.

"And having food and raiment let us be therewith content.

But they that will be rich fall into temptation and a snare, and into many foolish and hurtful lusts, which drown men in destruction and perdition.

For the love of money is the root of all evil: which while some coveted after, they have erred from the faith, and pierced themselves through with many sorrows.

But thou, O man of God, flee these things; and follow after righteousness, godliness, faith, love, patience, meekness."

I Timothy 6:8-11

 # Laws of Motion

"And the earth was without form, and void; and darkness was upon the face of the deep. And the Spirit of God moved upon the face of the waters.

And God said, Let there be light: and there was light.

And God saw the light, that it was good: and God divided the light from the darkness.

And God called the light Day, and the darkness he called Night. And the evening and the morning were the first day.

And God said, Let there be a firmament in the midst of the waters, and let it divide the waters from the waters.

And God made the firmament, and divided the waters which were under the firmament from the waters which were above the firmament: and it was so.

And God called the firmament Heaven. And the evening and the morning were the second day.

And God said, Let the waters under the heaven be gathered together unto one place, and let the dry land appear: and it was so."

Genesis 1:2-9

124

When we try to think about the universe we live in, we must think about *space, time,* and *matter. Space* is the word we use to mean where something is in the natural world. Since everything real has height and width and depth, we say space has three *dimensions.*

Time refers to the past, the present, and the future. Only man must think of events as being on this line somewhere; to God, the Bible says, one day is as a thousand years, and a thousand years are as one day (II Pet. 3:8). *Matter* refers to all the material in the universe–the stars, the planets, the rain, the animals, your coat, the book you are holding, your breath, everything. Matter is anything that takes up space and has weight.

What Is Motion?

To study *motion,* we must observe how the object (matter) changes position (space) during a certain period (time). Then we can go on to describe the motion–we can measure speed and distance and changes in speed.

If you see a car go by, you cannot say anything about its movement without referring to time, space, and matter. If you say it went by slowly, you had to judge that speed somehow, probably by comparing the time it took that car to go by with the time it usually takes a car to go by. Can you explain how time, space, and matter are all involved in that comparison?

Galileo Galilei and Isaac Newton, two scientists who studied motion, began to believe that if objects could be left entirely alone–no forces acting on them at all–that they would either be completely still or moving at a constant rate in a straight line. They called this theory *natural motion.* A comet, for example, if alone in the universe, could probably travel at a certain speed straight across the open space. What causes comets to slow down, speed up, and change course?

First Law of Motion

The idea that objects at rest tend to stay at rest and objects in motion tend to stay in motion is *Newton's first law* of motion. In science, a *law* is a statement that is made after many observations of the same event. How is a law different from a theory?

The resistance to a change from moving to not moving or from not moving to moving is called *inertia*. The term comes from a word that means "idleness." How does that definition seem appropriate? Have you ever been in a car that stopped suddenly? What happened? You probably were thrown forward. Why? Because your body was in motion, it tended to stay in motion after the car stopped. You demonstrated inertia. How do seatbelts in a car affect inertia?

If you push someone on a swing, is it easier to get him started or to keep him going? Probably it is harder to get him going because you must overcome his tendency to stay at rest.

Finding Out . . .

About Inertia

1. Get six checkers, a ruler, a small block of wood, a sheet of notebook paper, and a table with a smooth top.

2. Place the six checkers in a single stack on the table. Lay the ruler flat on the table about a foot from the stack. Then swiftly whisk the ruler into the bottom checker, sweeping it out from under the stack. What happens to the other five checkers? Why?

3. Put the sheet of paper at the edge of the table so that two-thirds hangs off the table. Place the wood block on the paper at the edge of the table. Hold the paper so that it makes a slight dip between your hand and the table edge. Then strike the paper in the dip smartly with the ruler. What happens to the block? Why?

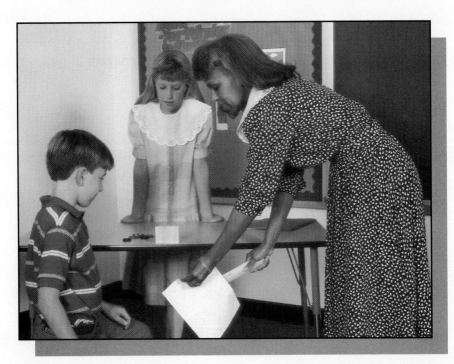

Second Law of Motion

Which is easier to throw—a softball or a shot-put?
Why? Part of *Newton's second law* of motion says that it
is easier to change the speed and direction of a light object
than a heavy one. Why do you think this is so?

Suppose you had to throw a life preserver to someone
who was far out in the water. How would you throw it?
Nice and easy? As hard as you could? You would throw it
as hard as you could. Why? The other part of the second
law says that the more force you use, the faster you can
change an object's speed and direction.

Can you explain why race cars are built light and have
powerful engines? Can you name some things that you
might do to help yourself run faster in a race?

Finding Out . . .

About Newton's Second Law

1. Get a strong magnet, a metal toy truck, several glass marbles, and a ruler.

2. Put the ruler on the table. Put the truck at one end of the ruler and the magnet at the other. Slowly push the magnet toward the toy until the toy begins to move. When the truck moves, stop pushing the magnet. Record where the truck began to move.

3. Put as many marbles in the truck as you can. Repeat the previous steps. What differences do you see?

Newton's Third Law

Why do you think your teacher says that there is to be no shoving when you line up? What happens if someone pushes the person in front of him? The person he pushes bumps into the person in front of him. And then what happens? The chain reaction that happens is one demonstration of *Newton's third law*. That law states that every action has an equal and opposite reaction.

Do you remember how rockets are propelled into space? How do rockets demonstrate Newton's third law of motion? When you blow up a balloon and let it go, what happens to the balloon? Can you explain how the balloon's movement and the rocket's movement are alike?

Can you describe the actions and reactions shown in these pictures?

Finding Out . . .

About Actions and Reactions

1. Get two rulers, seven dimes, and some modeling clay.

2. Put the rulers on a smooth surface. Be sure that the rulers are lying flat and parallel to each other about an inch apart. Secure both rulers to the table with modeling clay.

3. Beginning 1 inch from the end of the track between the rulers, line up five dimes, making sure that each coin touches the next. Then put one dime at the opening of the track, about an inch back from the line of dimes. Flick the dime into the other dimes straight on. What happens?

4. Set up the dimes again. Ask your science partner to put his finger on the fourth dime in line. Flick your dime into the line. What happens this time? Set up the dimes again. This time put two dimes touching each other at the opening. Flick both together into the line of dimes. What happens? Can you explain what happens by using Newton's third law?

Forces Influencing Motion

Since things in the universe do not remain still or keep moving in a straight line, there must be forces operating against natural motion. Think of throwing a softball toward home plate. What forces do you think keep the ball from traveling on over the backstop, over the bleachers, and out of the state?

Gravity

One force that keeps an object from traveling indefinitely is *gravity,* the pull of one body on another. Since the earth is larger than anything on it, it pulls objects toward itself. The softball, no matter how hard you throw it (unless you can throw it more than 25,000 miles an hour), will be pulled to the earth by this force we call gravity.

If you could go into space and throw the softball, what do you think would happen? Why do you think that? What do you think might cause a change in the path of the ball?

Friction

Friction is a rubbing force between two objects. It can both help and hinder movement. Without friction, we could not walk, for example. When you are standing, gravity pulls down on you and the floor pushes up on you. These forces balance each other; you do not fall down, nor do you get lifted up. To move, you must put the forces out of balance.

Your leg muscles change the position of your foot and exert a force down and back. Now friction helps: friction keeps your foot from sliding in the direction your leg is pushing. So the action of your leg now has the reaction of moving you forward. The muscles of your leg create such a strong force that the forces holding you still are put out of balance.

Think of yourself on wet ice. What would happen when your leg exerted force down and back? Your foot would probably keep going. Why? The forces have been put out of balance, but something crucial is missing. What? Why do some ice skates have ridges at the tip of the blades?

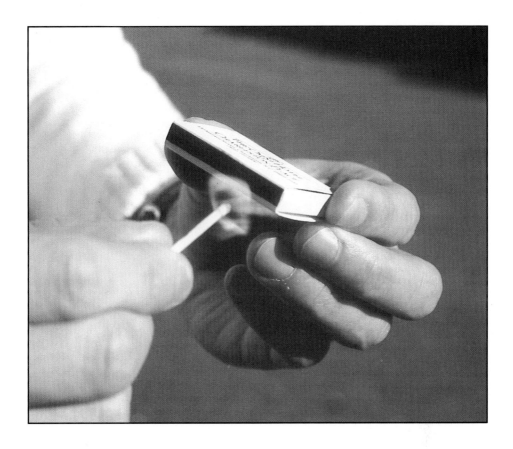

Friction that stops unwanted motion, such as falling on the ice, is called *traction*. Can you think of places that need traction? How is it produced in these places?

Friction is useful in other ways as well. You cannot strike a match without it. You need it to push your chair up to the supper table, and to turn over in bed. Can you think of other things friction helps you do?

Many times, however, friction is not helpful. Friction wears out tires, causes door hinges to squeak, creates holes in the pavement. It also makes holes in the knees of pants, gives you rope burns in a game of tug of war, and produces scuff marks on the kitchen floor. What are some things that people do to reduce friction?

Rolling friction results when one object rolls over another. If you roll a big ball to your little brother, you are using this kind of friction. Sliding friction is produced when two surfaces pass over or beside each other. When you raise a window, you use sliding friction. Flowing friction happens between two liquids or two gases; it also happens between a moving liquid or gas and a solid object. When you go swimming in the ocean, you create a flowing friction.

What kind of friction do you often see in a bowling alley? What friction occurs between your bicycle tires and the road? What kind of friction is involved when someone puts gasoline into his car? What kind of friction happens when an airplane flies through the clouds? What friction do you produce when you draw a line with a ruler?

Have you ever been in a strong wind and found it hard to walk? Air resistance was holding you back. What kind of friction is air resistance? Can you think of ways that airplane designers try to reduce flowing friction?

Friction creates heat. If you rub your hands back and forth together, you can feel the heat generated. When a spacecraft comes back into Earth's atmosphere, its outside temperature may increase to about five hundred degrees hotter than the melting point of iron. What precautions do builders of spacecrafts take against such friction?

INSIDE Information

Air resistance is not all bad. If raindrops met no resistance, for example, they would be falling faster than the speed of sound by the time they reached the earth. Rain showers would be painful indeed! Gravity pulls the drops earthward; air resistance slows them down. The two forces soon balance each other, and the drops fall at a constant speed. Can you think of other times when air resistance is useful? Would a parachutist do well without it?

When God created space and time and all matter, He set boundaries within which the world we know must operate. He established time and divided it; He created order and maintains it; He spoke forth the solar systems and fashioned our Earth and each of us to His own pleasure. It is one of our pleasures to study and describe what He has done.

Finding Out . . .

About Air Resistance

1. Get a square silk scarf, some string, several small weights or toys, and a pair of scissors.

2. Cut two pieces of string that are three times as long as one side of the scarf. Tie the ends of one string to two corners of the scarf (the corners must be on the same side, not opposite). Cut a small piece of string and tie the weight or toy to the "parachute" strings.

3. Fold the scarf in quarters and put the weight, strings untangled, on it. Then throw it into the air, or drop it from an upper-story window. What happens? Try different weights until you find the one that works best. Can you explain why it works best?

8

Nuclear Energy

When many people think of nuclear energy, they think of the first time such power was used as a weapon on the Japanese cities Hiroshima and Nagasaki at the end of World War II. Other people think of the nuclear power plants, where some of the electricity for our nation is generated. Nearly everyone knows something about what nuclear energy *can do.* But few really know what nuclear energy *is,* or that there are different kinds. And even fewer stop to think that every person in the world depends on some kind of nuclear reaction every day. What kind of nuclear reaction do you think everyone on the earth benefits from?

Energy from an Atom

An atom is the smallest part of any element that still can be recognized as that element. The smaller parts of the atom–electrons, neutrons, and protons–combine in different ways to form the atoms that make up everything in the universe.

Every atom has a *nucleus,* a center made of protons and neutrons. In "orbit" on different levels around the nucleus are electrons. It is the number of protons that an atom has that makes it different from all other kinds of atoms. For example, an atom of gold has seventy-nine protons. No other kind of atom has that particular arrangement.

Materials that are made of only one kind of atom are called *elements.* Gold is an element. What can you say about all its atoms?

INSIDE Information

Scientists now believe that there are more than two hundred different parts in the nucleus of an atom—parts smaller than the neutrons, protons, and electrons. These particles have names that sound more like science fiction than science: *mesons* and *pions* to list two.

HEY, A **STRANGE** THING HAPPENED TO ME ON THE WAY TO THE NUCLEUS ... I STOPPED FOR A BITE TO EAT AND GOT **PION** MY FACE. YUK-YUK!—HEY, ITS THE **TRUTH** ... BUT THE WORST PART IS—THE PIE GAVE ME **ATOMIC** ACHE — YUK-YUK! HEY—AND DID YOU HEAR ABOUT THE DUCK WHO SWALLOWED A PROTON?—IT MADE HIM **QUARK**. YUK-YUK!

ANOTHER STRANGE GREEN

The latest idea about atoms says that the particles are made of even smaller parts called *quarks.* The quarks come in different sizes and have different electrical charges. The different kinds of quarks are divided into *flavors* (the term here has nothing to do with taste): *up, down, strange, charm, truth,* and *beauty.*

Every flavor of quark belongs to one of three groups—*red, blue,* or *green.* (Once again, the name has nothing to do with the color of the quark.) Right now, there would seem to be eighteen different quarks, little particles with names like *truth red* and *up green.*

Finding Out . . .

About Electrons

1. Get some chloride salts of copper, lithium, and calcium, some table salt, some salt substitute, wooden splints or tongue depressors, and a Bunsen burner. You will also need a glass of distilled water.

2. Soak the wooden splints in water about twelve hours. Only when your teacher allows, adjust the Bunsen burner until the flame is blue or colorless.

3. Put a soaked splint into one of the salts. When several crystals stick to the splint, watch as your teacher holds the tip of the splint in the flame for a few seconds. (The wood will not burn for several seconds.) Be sure to watch the crystals constantly.

4. Record the name of the salt and the color it produced. Repeat the procedure for the other salts.

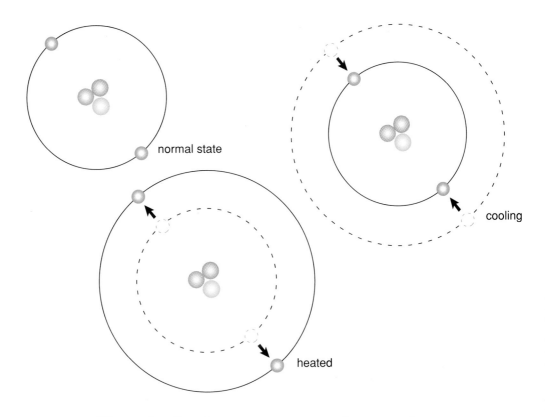

normal state

cooling

heated

The study of nuclear energy rests on what we understand of the atom. Many discoveries had to be made about how atoms are put together before we could understand that energy can come from them. A man named Niels Bohr discovered that when each element is heated and allowed to cool, it glows with its own combination of colors; no two elements glow alike. Bohr theorized that electrons move away from the nucleus when the atom is heated, that is, when it gains energy. When the energy is removed, the electrons return to their normal place. As they move back, they give off the light energy we see as color.

Because each element glows with its own set of colors, Bohr believed that each had its own arrangement of electrons. The special colors result as the electrons move back to unique levels in the different atoms. Bohr's discovery helped lead to others. Even now, scientists are learning new things about the tiny, mighty atom.

143

Sometimes atoms which have the same number of protons and electrons have different numbers of neutrons. These special atoms are called *isotopes*. The most common isotope of hydrogen, for example, has one proton, one electron, and no neutrons; but because it has other forms, it is an isotope. Another isotope of hydrogen has one proton, one electron, and one neutron. A third isotope has one proton, one electron, and two neutrons. Many elements have two or more forms.

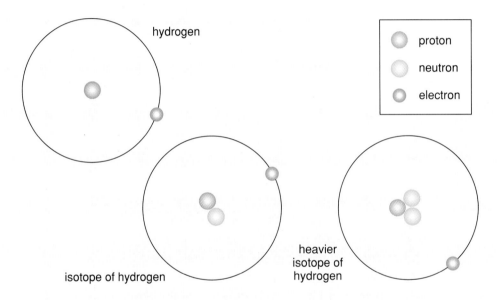

hydrogen

proton

neutron

electron

isotope of hydrogen

heavier
isotope of
hydrogen

Some isotopes do not hold together well, because they have too much energy. These isotopes give off particles and energy in a process called *radioactivity.*

Another way that some isotopes can give off extra energy is by splitting apart. Isotopes of uranium, for example, can go through this process. The nucleus splits apart into two or more pieces. Can you see where nuclear energy gets its name? When atoms split this way, we call it *fission.* When fission happens, energy is released. Nuclear power plants can cause fission in certain fuels and put the energy to use.

Nuclear Power Plants

The center of the nuclear power plant is the *reactor*. A reactor is a machine that allows the fissioning of uranium to be controlled. It holds a combination of uranium isotopes that can be split easily and of materials that can slow down the splitting process.

Atoms that undergo fission are also used in nuclear weapons. It is impossible for the fuel that is used in a nuclear reactor to be made to explode like a bomb. Why is that important? Weapons use a different fuel and a faster reaction.

The fuel, the material that releases neutrons, keeps atomic reactions going. Materials that can absorb the free neutrons are used as *control rods*. If all the control rods are put into the reactor, the nuclear fission will slow down and stop. Why is that? What do you think happens as the control rods are slowly taken out of the reactor?

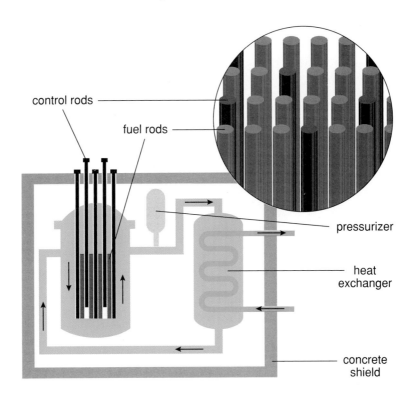

control rods

fuel rods

pressurizer

heat exchanger

concrete shield

The fission produces tremendous amounts of heat. The heat is used to turn water into steam. The steam is then used to power a generator that creates electricity. One pellet of uranium fuel about the size of the eraser on a new pencil can produce as much energy as about 1 ton of coal or nearly 160 gallons (600 liters) of oil.

Nuclear reactors cost many millions of dollars to build. Why do you think that is so? Also the people who work there have to have much special training. Still many think that the gains in power are worth the cost. What reasons do you think they give?

Nuclear Station

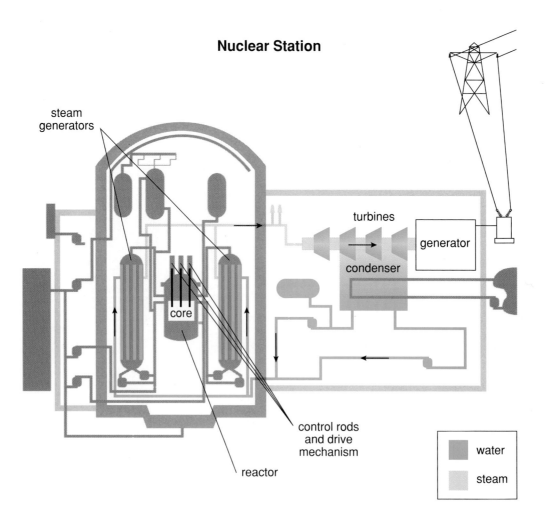

Reactor Operating

Many people must work together with precision and care to keep a nuclear power plant running safely and efficiently. Among others, there are mechanical technicians, chemists, geologists, and reactor operators. Senior reactor operators supervise all other operators in a nuclear power plant.

To become a *nuclear operator,* a person must study mathematics, nuclear science, physics, and other subjects. Then the student begins to learn basic procedures at a nuclear plant. After that, if he wants an operator's license and has passed the tests, the student begins training in a *simulator,* a room that is an exact copy of the control room of a nuclear plant.

Finally the student must pass several long and difficult tests on how both the reactor and the power plant work in order to get a license from the U.S. Nuclear Regulatory Commission. To become a *senior reactor operator,* the operator must study even more and gain experience in the control of a plant. All operators, even seniors, must pass a test every two years to keep their licenses. Why do you think the training and testing are as difficult as they are?

Finding Out . . .

About Nuclear Reactors

1. Get a glass beaker, some rusted iron filings, some hydrogen peroxide, and a strong bar magnet.

2. Pour enough hydrogen peroxide into the beaker to cover half the magnet. Without the magnet in the beaker, sprinkle enough filings into the peroxide to get a good reaction going. What part of the operation of a nuclear reaction does this action represent?

3. Slowly lower the magnet into the beaker. What happens? What does the magnet represent? As you pull the magnet out, scrape the filings off. What happens then? Draw and label the parts of the "reactor."

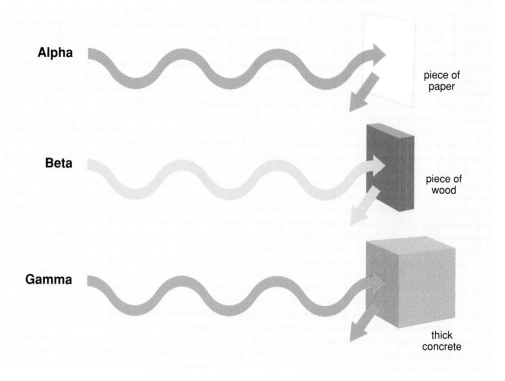

Alpha — piece of paper

Beta — piece of wood

Gamma — thick concrete

Radiation

When atoms are losing parts, they give off *alpha particles, beta particles,* or *gamma rays.* The alpha and beta particles are streams of tiny bits of matter from the nucleus of the atom. Gamma rays are made of waves of energy released during radioactivity. The particles and energy given off during radioactivity are called *radiation.*

The alpha particles can be turned aside by a piece of paper. The beta particles can be stopped by wood or tinfoil. But it takes a thick wall of concrete or lead to stop the gamma ray. Which do you think is the most difficult to protect against?

Uranium goes through fission in nature and produces two different materials. However, in nature the change happens slowly, and the radiation is small. Can you think how natural radioactivity differs from the radioactivity produced in a nuclear reactor?

In the United States, the reactors are encased in buildings with concrete walls more than 3 feet thick and concrete floors more than 8 feet thick. All the concrete is reinforced with steel rods. Inside the concrete wall is a steel shell nearly $\frac{1}{2}$ inch thick on all sides and across the top and bottom. These concrete and steel walls make up the *containment building*.

The nuclear reactor itself is inside a steel case that has walls $8\frac{1}{2}$ inches thick. That case is surrounded by concrete walls 3 to 5 feet thick, all reinforced with steel.

INSIDE Information

The accident at the nuclear power plant in Chernobyl in the Soviet Union happened because operators attempted a test under improper conditions. As a result, the reactor went to five hundred times its normal full power level. Chemicals in the reactor exploded. Radioactive particles got into the air by the explosion and the fire that followed. Why is it especially bad when radioactive particles get into the open air?

The reactor was inside a building with walls no thicker than the walls of an ordinary factory building. And Chernobyl's reactors are very different from those at power plants in the rest of the world. This accident could happen only in a plant like Chernobyl. Their rules left room for operators to make such a mistake. Since then the Soviets have joined the World Association of Nuclear Operators.

United States Nuclear Building

Chernobyl Nuclear Building

steel:
nearly 1/2 in. thick
8 1/2 in. thick

concrete, 3 ft. thick

steel container

graphite

concrete

fuel rods

steel-reinforced concrete:
5 ft. thick
4 ft. thick
3 ft., 9 in. thick
8 ft., 6 in. thick

unreinforced concrete:
regular building thickness
about 6 ft. thick

bedrock

Some people have the idea that all radioactivity is produced by man and is harmful. Neither assumption is true. In nature, radioactivity occurs in radium, for example. The radium atoms break down slowly, becoming other materials. By handling hundreds of pounds of ore, Marie Curie, a scientist of the early 1900s, may have been exposed to enough radiation to have caused her illness and death. Normally a person would not be exposed to enough radium in his lifetime to cause him any harm.

On the other hand, some artificially caused radiation is not harmful. If you have ever seen a wind-up clock that glows in the dark, you have seen a useful, harmless result of radiation. Why do you think it is not harmful? It is harmless because there is not much radiation.

Glow-in-the-dark clocks have numbers that are coated with paint containing zinc sulfide and radium or tritium. The radium breaks down, sending out radiations that cause little bursts of light when they hit the zinc sulfide.

Radioactivity in nature can be detected with a meter called a *Geiger counter,* a machine that counts the number of rays or particles that strike its sensor.

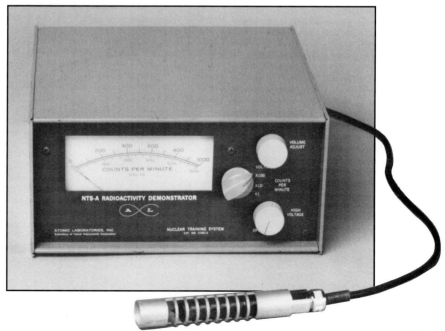

Finding Out . . .

About Radiation

1. Get a clock that glows in the dark and a magnifying glass. You will also need a place that can be made completely dark.

2. Go into a dark room and wait until your eyes adjust to the darkness. Then hold the clock close to your eyes until you can see the tiny flashes coming from the numbers.

3. Look at the flashes with a magnifying glass. Can you explain what may be causing the flashes? Draw a diagram of what you think is happening.

Nuclear Medicine

Radiation can be used to help people. The branch of medicine that uses different kinds of radiation to detect or treat disease is called *nuclear medicine*. Using isotopes that break up easily and quickly, medical technicians can direct the radiation that is given off to kill cancer cells.

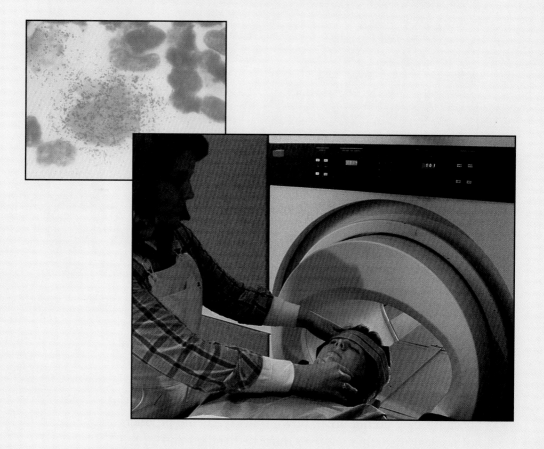

Other isotopes can be injected into the blood and then traced by special machines–something like Geiger counters for the body. For example, when isotopes reach the brain of a patient, a machine can follow the pattern the blood makes as it flows over the brain. The tracings can reveal a problem, like a blood clot or a tumor.

153

Too much radiation is harmful, however. Workers in nuclear plants wear special coveralls and carry meters to sample the air and test for radioactivity. Especially dangerous are the fuels that have been used in nuclear reactors. These waste products are highly radioactive. And because they do not break down quickly, as the products of nuclear medicine do, they must be handled and stored carefully. Exposure to that much radiation can seriously harm or even kill a person.

Yet nuclear power plants have a remarkable safety record. In the twenty-five years that the 1,000 plants have been running in the United States, no one has been killed or injured in a radiation accident.

Finding Out . . .

About Geiger Counters

1. Get a Geiger counter or a radioactivity indicator, a clock that glows in the dark, a piece of uranium ore from a rock collection, and two other objects of your choice for testing. Or you may choose to get a roll of unexposed film and a piece of uranium ore.

2. Bring the clock near the Geiger counter. Record what happens. Bring the ore and the other objects near the counter. Record your findings each time.

3. What can you say about the atoms in each object?

4. If you have unexposed film, place it in a drawer with the uranium ore. Leave the drawer closed for two days. Then remove the film and develop it. What do you see?

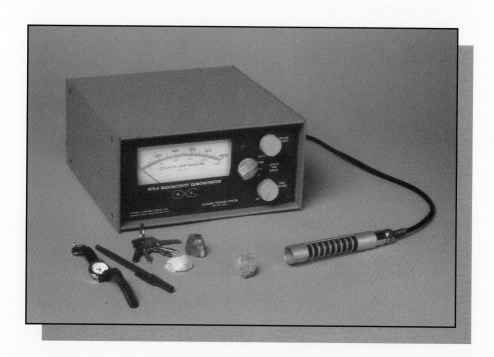

Other Choices

Some scientists think that in the future we can copy the way the sun generates energy rather than depending on fission. Instead of atoms splitting to release energy, atoms on the sun are under such pressure that they combine. This process is called *fusion,* and it releases great amounts of energy. If men can cause fusion such as occurs in the sun, what problems do you think they can avoid that come with fission? What new problems do you think they might encounter? For one thing, the heat that is generated on the sun would evaporate any material we know of on the earth. The problem would be to build a place that could contain the fusion.

Why do men keep looking for new ways of producing energy? Many fear that we are running out of fuels such as coal and oil. Others fear the nuclear energy plants, thinking that their effects will not all be known for years to come. The Christian, while recognizing his responsibility to use the treasures God has given him in the earth properly, need not fear the future as many others do. He can view events from another perspective, one that acknowledges God's ultimate control.

"Declaring the end from the beginning, and from ancient times the things that are not yet done, saying, My counsel shall stand, and I will do all my pleasure."

Isaiah 46:10

 Chemistry

A few hundred years ago, a man named Daniel von Siebenburgen arrived in Florence, Italy, with a new drug he called *usafur*. He went around town and sold the drug, a combination of a little gold and much mercury, to every apothecary. Then, some time later, Daniel went to see the ruler of Florence, promising a most surprising thing: he would turn a common drug into pure gold.

Daniel told the ruler that he knew how to bring gold from the cheap drug usafur. The ruler doubted such a thing could be done, but he ordered his men to go to any apothecary in Florence and bring back some usafur. This they did, and by heating the medicine, Daniel was able every time to produce gold. But it was not long before Florence ran out of usafur. What do you think happened then? Daniel volunteered to go to France and get some more. The ruler gave him a huge sum of money and gladly sent him off to France. And Daniel was never seen in Florence again.

Such is the story of a greedy man who tricked other greedy men into giving him money. His success was partly due to a notion that had been held for a long time. It was thought that with the proper formula, gold could easily be made from lesser metals. For centuries men spent their lives trying every combination of metals and liquids in the vain search for easy wealth. These searchers we call *alchemists*.

Not all alchemists were tricksters; some studied and experimented to uncover how one substance could be changed into another. Others went in search of a potion that would help them live forever. Many of the experimenters invented amazing new products, like waterproof cloth and painkillers and glow-in-the-dark ink. But these inventions were usually tossed aside as miserable failures in the quest for riches. One young alchemist, however, found a better way to make porcelain—and he gave up alchemy and turned to porcelain making.

One good result that all this effort led to was the true science of chemistry. *Chemistry* is the study of the different kinds of matter—what they are made of, how they react to other matter, what their usual characteristics are. True chemistry does not rest on false hopes or clever tricks but rather on careful investigation and accurate recording.

Properties of Matter

All matter has its own particular characteristics or *properties*. Water, for example, boils at 212° F (100° C); rubbing alcohol will boil at just over 165° F (78° C). A property of water is its boiling point; a property of alcohol is its boiling point.

Physical Properties

A *physical property* is one that you can observe or measure without changing the *kind* of matter you are studying. You can observe that a ruby is red and that a diamond is hard. You can tell whether it is a roast or fried chicken in the kitchen by the smell. Color, hardness, and odor are physical properties.

The *state* or form of matter is another physical property. All matter is either *solid, liquid,* or *gas.* A tennis shoe has a physical property of being a solid. What can you say about an inflated balloon? The balloon itself is a solid; it is filled with a gas. The balloon has one physical property, and the gas has another.

Chemical Properties

A *chemical property* is one that you can observe only when the matter you are studying reacts with other matter and changes into a new kind of matter. When iron meets oxygen, for instance, a reaction between them often produces a new material–rust. The tendency of iron to rust is one of its chemical properties.

Chrome is a metal that does not rust. What is one of its chemical properties? Can you think of some places where chrome is used? Why do you think it is used in those places?

Changes in Matter

Matter does not stay the same all the time. Clothes wear out; perfume evaporates; food is digested; ponds freeze over; ice cream melts. Some changes simply cause the matter to take a different form. Other changes completely alter the matter, making it something different from what it was.

Physical Changes

If matter changes shape or state but remains the same kind of matter, we say it has had a *physical change*. If you pluck a daisy from its stem, you have changed the plant's shape–but it is a daisy still.

If you boil water, you change its state from liquid to gas–but the water is still water. The only difference is that you have caused the water molecules to spread apart so much that the water is now floating in the air rather than being contained in the pan.

Is ice still water? Yes, it is. What state is it in? What about the butter that melts on your blueberry muffin? Is it still butter? Why do you say so? Do you think that the sawdust from a piece of wood is still wood?

Chemical Changes

When matter is made into some other kind of matter by a change, that change is *chemical*. If you burn a piece of wood, do you still have wood? No, you have ashes, a different kind of matter. A chemical change has taken place. Many chemical reactions go on all around you and inside you every day.

When you breathe in, your body takes in oxygen that combines with digested food to produce energy. Before that, the food you ate was combined with other substances in your body, such as saliva, so that digestion could go on. Every time someone starts a bus or a car, fuel and oxygen coming together cause a chemical change. Every time it rains, the rainwater reacts with minerals in rocks and soil, breaking down bits of rock and enriching the soil.

In a chemical change, the atoms themselves are not altered; they just get rearranged to form a different matter. How then is a chemical reaction different from a nuclear reaction?

What clues are there that a chemical change has taken place? Many chemical reactions create heat. Others are caused by heat. If no heat is used or produced, then it is not likely that a chemical change happened. Does the production or use of heat always mean a chemical change has taken place? No, it does not. Ice, you recall, melts when heat is added but does not chemically change.

In many chemical reactions there is a color change. Can you think of a physical change that causes a color change? How about mixing grape drink mix with water? In some other reactions, a gas is released. Can you use a result as a clue about the kind of change if it does not happen in almost every reaction? What cautions should you take in naming a change physical or chemical?

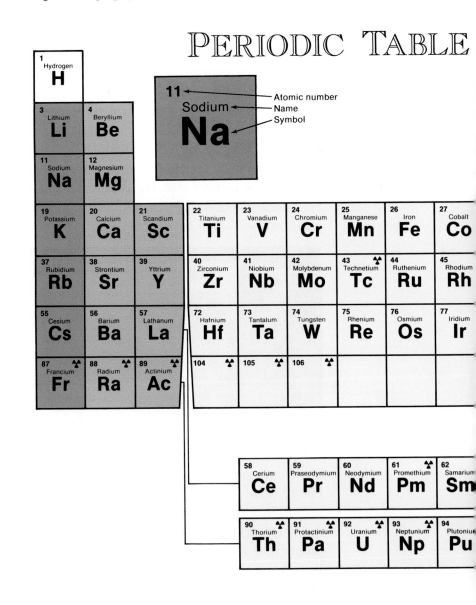

PERIODIC TABLE

To show what they believe is happening in a chemical change, scientists use codes or *chemical symbols.* The symbols are arranged into *formulas,* or equations, that anyone who knows the symbols can read. Look at the chart to read the formula describing how iron rusts.

$$4\ Fe \quad + \quad 3\ O_2 \quad \rightarrow \quad 2\ Fe_2O_3$$

four atoms of iron   six atoms (bonded into   yields   rust
three molecules) of oxygen

OF THE ELEMENTS

					2 Helium **He**
5 Boron **B**	6 Carbon **C**	7 Nitrogen **N**	8 Oxygen **O**	9 Fluorine **F**	10 Neon **Ne**
13 Aluminum **Al**	14 Silicon **Si**	15 Phosphorus **P**	16 Sulfur **S**	17 Chlorine **Cl**	18 Argon **Ar**

28 Nickel **Ni**	29 Copper **Cu**	30 Zinc **Zn**	31 Gallium **Ga**	32 Germanium **Ge**	33 Arsenic **As**	34 Selenium **Se**	35 Bromine **Br**	36 Krypton **Kr**
46 Palladium **Pd**	47 Silver **Ag**	48 Cadmium **Cd**	49 Indium **In**	50 Tin **Sn**	51 Antimony **Sb**	52 Tellurium **Te**	53 Iodine **I**	54 Xenon **Xe**
78 Platinum **Pt**	79 Gold **Au**	80 Mercury **Hg**	81 Thallium **Tl**	82 Lead **Pb**	83 Bismuth **Bi**	84 Polonium **Po**	85 Astatine **At**	86 Radon **Rn**

63 Europium **Eu**	64 Gadolinium **Gd**	65 Terbium **Tb**	66 Dysprosium **Dy**	67 Holmium **Ho**	68 Erbium **Er**	69 Thulium **Tm**	70 Ytterbium **Yb**	71 Lutetium **Lu**
95 Americium **Am**	96 Curium **Cm**	97 Berkelium **Bk**	98 Californium **Cf**	99 Einsteinium **Es**	100 Fermium **Fm**	101 Mendelevium **Md**	102 Nobelium **No**	103 Lawrencium **Lw**

Finding Out . . .

About Chemical Changes

1. Get some marble powder (calcium carbonate), some water, an eyedropper, two beakers, a test tube, a filter paper, a small jar with a lid, and a drinking straw.

2. Put about 6 milliliters (about $\frac{1}{2}$ tsp.) of calcium carbonate into a beaker. Describe the substance. Add three or four drops of water. What happens? Has a chemical change taken place? Why do you say so? The beaker now contains *slaked lime,* or *quicklime* (calcium hydroxide).

3. Make some more slaked lime in the jar, and seal the lid tightly. You will need this compound for another activity later.

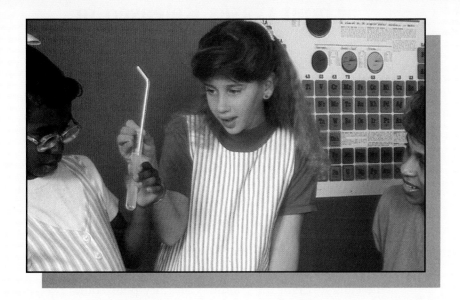

4. Add 200 milliliters of water to the slaked lime in the beaker. Pour the liquid through the filter into another beaker. The slaked lime is now *limewater*. Pour about one-fourth of the limewater into a test tube. Hold the drinking straw in the tube, being careful not to let the straw touch the limewater. Blow gently into the straw. (DO NOT DRAW YOUR BREATH IN; LIME-WATER WILL BURN YOU.) What happens to the limewater? Has there been a chemical change? From what you know about respiration, can you say what gas you breathe out? Calcium carbonate has formed again. What substances reacted to form the calcium carbonate?

5. Let the rest of the limewater stand uncovered in the beaker for a few days. Record any changes that occur. What do your observations seem to indicate about the air in the beaker?

Finding Out . . .

About Gases Released in Chemical Reactions

1. Get some vinegar, some baking soda, a short candle, a match, a glass jar that is taller than the candle, a lid for the jar, some limewater, and a saucer.

2. Fix the candle upright on the saucer. Light the candle. Put the open jar upside down over it until it goes out. Quickly lift the jar, pour in some limewater, and put on the lid. Shake the water briefly. What happens? What does this tell you about the air in the jar?

3. Wash out the jar and fix the candle upright in the bottom. Pour in some baking soda around the base of the candle. Light the candle. Carefully pour some vinegar onto the soda in the jar. What happens? What happens to the candle? What do you think caused the candle to go out? What does that tell you about the reaction between the vinegar and the soda?

Elements, Mixtures, and Compounds

All the substances in the world can be put into one of three groups. Any substance that is made of only one kind of atom is an *element*. Gold, you remember, is an element. It is made only of gold atoms. A *mixture* is a combination of two (or more) different substances. The combination must involve only physical changes, however, to be a mixture.

If you throw red checkers and black checkers into a box together, you have created a mixture. If you add sugar to tea, you have created a mixture. How do you know? The sweetness of the sugar goes throughout the tea, and even though the tea then tastes sweet, the tea is still tea and the sugar is still sugar.

Some mixtures are easy to separate; some are not. How long do you think it would take you to put the red checkers in one pile and the black ones in another? Could you get the sugar out of the tea? Can you explain why the best way to tell a mixture is by how its parts keep their own identities?

"And there came also Nicodemus, which at the first came to Jesus by night, and brought a mixture of myrrh and aloes, about an hundred pound weight."

John 19:39

Finding Out . . .

About Mixtures

1. Get 50 milliliters of iron filings, 100 milliliters of sulfur, a glass pan, a wooden dowel or spoon, and a magnet.

2. Stir the filings and the sulfur together thoroughly in the pan with the dowel or spoon handle. Is this a mixture? Why do you say so?

3. Think of some ways to separate the two elements. What way do you think is the fastest? Use the magnet to clean up.

4. Watch as your teacher mixes the elements again and heats them thoroughly. Describe the substance after it cools. How is its color different from the iron and the sulfur? Test it for magnetism. Is this a mixture? What do you base your answer on?

A *compound* is made when two or more different elements combine to make a new substance. What kind of change is required to make a compound? Is rust a compound? How do you know?

What do you think is the most common compound on the earth? It is a combination of oxygen and hydrogen, two gases that together make a liquid. That liquid is water, the compound that makes up most of your body and covers most of the earth. Why do you think that God has provided the earth with so much of this compound?

When elements combine chemically, they lose their individual properties. Salt, for instance, is made of a greenish, poisonous gas (chlorine) and a metal (sodium) that explodes when put with water. But together they make *sodium chloride,* which you sprinkle on your watermelon and popcorn and eat with pleasure and safety. In fact, a little salt is necessary to your health.

Finding Out . . .

About Mixtures and Compounds

1. Get 50 milliliters of plaster of Paris, 50 milliliters of potting soil or dirt, two beakers, some water, and a rod or spoon for stirring.

2. Put the plaster and the soil into separate beakers. Add a little water to each and stir until both become thick, somewhat like applesauce. Let the beakers stand for a few minutes.

3. Decide which beaker contains a compound and which contains a mixture. On what observations do you base your conclusions?

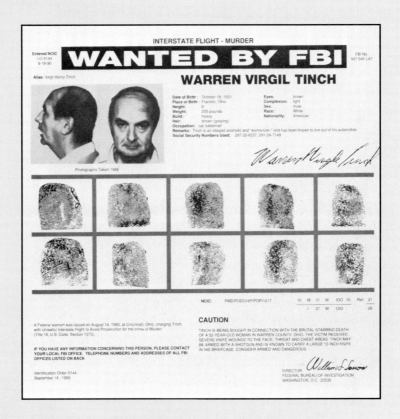

Criminal Investigation

There had been a burglary. The burglar came in through a broken window in the kitchen. He was frightened off before he stole anything, but he had been careful: he wiped off all hard surfaces and left nothing behind. He was gone without a trace. Or was he?

When the police were called, they sent two *forensics officers,* people trained in science and law, to investigate. They took photographs and made some sketches of the broken window and the turned-over flowerpot on the sill. They measured the hole in the glass and studied the jagged edges closely.

173

On one tiny shard of glass, the officers discovered what they thought might be dried blood. They carefully put the glass with the brown flakes into a sealable plastic bag. One officer found a hair, which he put into another bag. This could later be classified and compared to the hair of a suspect. The other officer discovered some papers jumbled in an open drawer. She quickly decided to seal those in a large bag as well.

After many hours of careful collecting and recording, the officers used a vacuum with a special filter to get up any threads or other fine material they might have missed. They would use a microscope and chemical tests to identify any fibers found. Why do you think they would want to do this? They aimed lights across surfaces to see any fingerprints, but the burglar seemed to have left none. Then the officers went back to their crime laboratory to study the evidence they had collected.

One officer used chemicals to find the type of blood on the window. It was *AB* positive. No member of the household or either detective had that type blood. They studied the photos and decided that the intruder must have just slightly scratched himself on the way out.

The other officer put a series of chemicals on the papers she had found, and in a short time, many fingerprints came into view. She photographed them and compared all the prints to the fingerprints of every member of the house. Most matched up. But on the bottom left of one sheet were two clear prints that were not made by anyone who lived in the house. At last, there was some definite proof that, careful as he was, the burglar had not gotten clean away.

What other science skills and knowledge did the officers use?

 # Animal Behavior

In some mild waters of the Pacific Ocean, a whale gives birth. The baby is 22 feet (6.4 m) long and weighs 3 tons. It looks small, though, beside its mother, an 85-foot (26-m) blue whale. In a dewy pasture in Tennessee, a mare nuzzles a newborn foal. In places all over the world, animals raise their young, search for food, hide from their enemies, call for mates, find water, sleep, stand guard–in short, live their whole lives according to the behaviors God has given them.

A baby whale comes into the world knowing how to swim. A mother horse automatically licks her newborn foal, which helps its breathing and circulation. God has given animals *instincts,* or impulses they are born with. God has also given some animals the ability to learn a behavior. *Learned behavior* usually results from trial and error or from teaching. The baby whale, although it knows how to swim, would have to be taught to jump out of the water on command. And although a horse knows how to care for a foal, it must learn to respond to the bit and reins.

God has designed animals to be able to make adjustments to conditions where they live. They can, if need be, move to an entirely different place, of course. But even if they stay in one area, most animals can change the way they do things to compensate for such adversities as prolonged dry weather, severe cold, or dwindling food supply. Animals sometimes undergo physical changes as well. Some grow thicker fur in cold weather. The arctic fox has a thick white coat in the winter to help it blend in with snowy surroundings. In summer, its coat changes to brown or gray. Such adjusting is often called *adaptation*.

Any adapting that animals do is limited by heredity; an animal that does not, for example, grow fur cannot develop that ability if the weather should suddenly turn cold. Only an animal that has the genes to grow more fur will do so. An animal can only use more or less of its God-given capabilities when conditions demand it. How does this fact contradict the theory of evolution?

In giving animals these instincts and abilities, God has provided for their survival. Each kind of animal has the equipment and the ability that it needs to get food and to produce more of its own kind.

Social Relationships

Survival requires food, water, oxygen, and space. Some animals, like bears, can take care of most of these needs by themselves, living alone most of the time. The jack rabbit, streamlined for speed, always lives alone. As soon as baby jack rabbits quit nursing, they are on their own. Other animals can survive only in groups, dividing up duties, territory, and food.

Animals of the same kind living together are called *animal populations*. Most animal populations have group names, and some even have group names depending on what the group is doing. For example, when geese are on the ground, they are a *flock;* in the air they are a *skein* or a *flight;* on the water they are a *gaggle.*

INSIDE Information

Group Names

bears	*sleuth, sloth*
cats	*clowder, clutter*
chicks	*brood, clutch*
crows	*murder*
elephants	*kindergarten*
elks	*gang*
fish	*draught, school, shoal*
foxes	*leash, skulk*
gnats	*cloud, horde*
goats	*tribe, trip*
goldfinches	*charm*
hares	*down, husk*
hawks	*cask*
hounds	*cry, mute, pack*
kangaroos	*troup*
larks	*exaltation*
leopards	*leap*

By living in groups many animals find it easier to defend themselves, to get food, to care for the young, to establish and keep territory, and to find mates. Wolves mate for life, take care of cubs until they are grown, and even care for old or injured members of their close family group. Wolves can work together to bring down an elk or even a moose that one wolf alone could not. Lions live in prides for the same reason: to share a zebra is better than trying to catch one alone.

Why do you think animals such as bears and tigers do not live in groups? When do you think these animals would live with others of their own kind for a time?

lions	*pride*
moles	*labor*
nightingales	*watch*
oysters	*bed*
peacocks	*muster*
pheasants	*nest, nide, nye*
plovers	*congregation, wing*
quails	*bevy, covey*
rabbits	*colony*
seals	*pod*
starlings	*murmuration*
toads	*knot*
turkeys	*rafter*
whales	*gam, pod*
wildfowl	*plump*
wolves	*pack*

Finding Out . . .

About Populations

1. Get your notebook and a pencil. Locate a population of animals, perhaps a flock of birds or a colony of ants.

2. Observe the population carefully. What do they do? What do they eat? How do they seem to communicate with each other? Can you count how many there are in the group?

3. Record as many observations as you can about the group. Write a report of your observations.

Some animals live together–but they are not the same kind. For example, a bird called the oxpecker lives among large animals like water buffaloes, eating the ticks that live on their hides. This kind of arrangement is *symbiosis,* a word that comes from *syn-* (''together'') and *bios* (''life''). What does the oxpecker gain by this symbiosis? What does the water buffalo gain?

Other animals of different kinds also live together, but the arrangement is usually harmful to one animal. Fleas, for example, live on dogs. The fleas benefit, drawing nourishment from the dog. The dog does not benefit; it loses blood, may get parasites, and has the annoyance of needing to scratch. Theirs is a *host-parasite* relationship; the dog is the host, the flea is the parasite. *Parasite* comes from *para* (''beside'') and *sitos* (''food''). How is the name fitting?

Communication

Whether living alone or in groups, animals communicate, mostly with others of their own kind. They use *behavior* (body signs), *sounds,* and *odors* to send messages.

Sometimes all of these methods of communicating are used at once. For example, when a fawn is born, the doe spends much time the first day or so nuzzling her new baby, sniffing it, snorting to it, licking it. The two are getting to know each other by sight, by sound, by touch, by smell, and even by taste. Later when the doe returns from grazing, she will be able to find her fawn, even though there may be many hidden in the same woods. And the fawn will know his mother and come out of hiding only for her. How does this behavior help the fawn?

Porpoises seem to have a complex language. They use whistles, clicks, and barks to communicate with each other. The humpback whales sing ''songs'' that can be recorded and studied by oceanographers. The songs travel through hundreds of miles of water to reach other whales, giving them news of the pod and of feeding places or dangers.

Yawning among animals is often a form of communication. Lizards and fish commonly threaten unwelcome visitors by yawning. Baboons establish ranking in the group by yawning, and lionesses yawn to distract potential enemies from their cubs. Polar bears yawning at each other indicate that their intentions are peaceful. Crocodiles, unable to move their tongues well enough to clean their teeth thoroughly, yawn, and birds are attracted to the leftovers.

Many animal groups like to designate a territory as theirs. Some patrol their boundaries, running off intruders. Many fight or make aggressive displays, defending an area that can be as small as a tern's nest or, in the case of the golden eagle, as large as 100 square kilometers. Others use scent marking to communicate that certain places have been claimed.

Courtship

Courtship makes use of many, and sometimes unusual, forms of communication in the animal kingdom. Peacocks show that they want mates by displaying their glorious feathers. Which of the three main methods of communication is the peacock using?

Many animals have a special sound, or mating call, that attracts members of the opposite sex. Turkey hunters use this information to their advantage, using a turkey call to get gobblers to come toward them. Storks, which lack voices, clatter with their beaks. Snipes make a bleating sound by spreading their tail feathers and letting the air rush through. Male crickets "fiddle" by scraping one wing across another. The male spruce grouse fans his tail feathers and drums the air with his wings to win a female.

Other birds have dances or struts they do to attract a mate. The European blackcock, for example, comes to the same place every year and dances as the females gather around to watch.

The bowerbird of New Guinea dances for his mate too, but first he has to get her attention by building a courtship house. Constructed of twigs and sticks and brightly decorated with berries, leaves, flowers, and feathers, these bowers are not used to raise young; they are only courting places. What methods of communication is the bowerbird using?

Some animals fight to show they want a mate. Young stallions in wild pony herds must challenge the lead stallion and win the fight to earn the right to approach the mares. Bull walruses, too, roar and batter into each other for the privilege of taking a mate.

Still other animals send signals. Some female animals, like white-tailed does, leave a different scent track when they would have the bucks approach them. Female fireflies send a special pattern of light signals that get the males' attention.

The roseate spoonbill picks up a stick and rattles it. The female ignores him until he struts closer and wags his head, waving the stick. Abruptly, he drops the stick at her feet and steps back. If she picks it up, the stick will be the first in their nest.

Warning

Courtship, however, is only one reason animals communicate. To warn of danger is an important reason too. If a beaver sees an enemy coming, it lifts its broad, flat tail and smacks it down on the water, making a sharp crack that can sometimes be heard a mile away. Any other beaver in hearing range dives under the water to safety.

Mother animals often grunt to or nudge their young when danger is near. Elephants, for example, pull the babies along with their trunks to get them safely in the circle of adults.

The skunk turns its back and raises its tail to warn an enemy, and the rattlesnake's rattle is a warning to stay away. The pika, a small short-eared relative of the rabbit, calls out in a kind of ventriloquism to warn other pikas of danger. Its whistle seems to come from a different place each time, and the tactic fools any would-be predators.

Piglike peccaries alert each other by giving off strong odors. The pronghorn antelope have signal flags on their hindquarters. These are white circular patches of hair. When an antelope sights trouble, it raises the patches. The hairs reflect light and make flashes that can be detected by other antelope as far as 4 miles (6.4 km) away.

Getting Food

Getting food is probably the single most important task for any animal. That search drives the animal almost constantly, for it can live without a mate, without space, and even a while without rest; but it cannot live long without food and water.

Honeybees coming upon a promising field of pollen and nectar return to the hive and perform an intricate "dance" that shows the other bees where the find is. Ants leave a scent trail that others can follow to food. Birds such as quail sometimes use a "gathering call" to get members of the flock together where there is food and safety.

Bats use the echoes from short, high squeaks, inaudible to humans, to detect objects. The sounds bounce off the objects back to the bats' ears. Bats, seemingly flying blind at night, use this process, called *echolocation*, to snare their food.

Some animals do not have to work very hard, although they must work nearly all the time, to get their food. Hydras, for instance, can stay attached to rocks and wait for currents to bring them food. Sponges must remain stationary, getting food from the water that flows around them. These animals feed by *reflex*, an inborn response to a change in the environment. When food touches the hydra, the animal responds by eating it. It does not think about eating the food; it just eats it.

Other animals must go after their food. The otter has to satisfy a huge appetite every day. The otter's diet includes spiny shellfish. The otter dives to the seafloor and returns with both a shellfish and a rock. Then it lies on its back in the water and uses the rock to crack open the shellfish. The walrus, another sea mammal that eats sea creatures from the seafloor, prefers clams. It feels along the seafloor with its long tusks and 400 sensitive whiskers. The walrus may weigh more than a ton and a half and may eat about 1,000 shellfish a day.

Some creatures have tongues that do all the food-catching. Faster than the eye can see, a chameleon whips out its tongue and snares an insect. The anteater, with a giant appetite for ants and termites, is not content to get them one at a time. Its 2-foot (61-cm) tongue is covered with a sticky substance to which insects adhere by the hundreds. Frogs and salamanders, with long tongues attached at the front of the mouth, are also able to capture insects.

Other animals scavenge, that is, eat dead or decaying material. They come behind the lions, the wolves, and the leopards, taking what is left, consuming what no other animal will eat. Some scavengers are vultures, hyenas, and certain kinds of beetles. How are such animals helpful?

Another fairly simple method for finding food is stealing. It can, however, be a little dangerous at times. A commando spider lives at the edge of a much larger spider's web, waiting to steal a catch. He must move carefully, gingerly over the web, so as not to alert the owner. Instead of stealing a meal, the commando might be one.

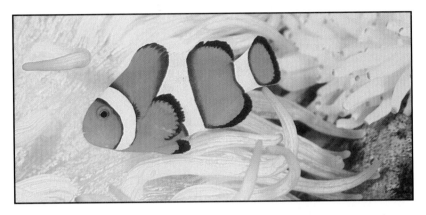

Other animals provide a service. The oxpecker, as mentioned before, eats insects on water buffaloes. It also benefits the zebras. This service keeps the zebras free of harmful pests and yields the oxpecker a good meal without much trouble. Another pair of animals living together and providing services for each other is the colorful clownfish and the stinging sea anemone. Although the sea anemone would hurt most other fish, the clownfish is able to reside among its tentacles. Protected there, the clownfish gets food and attracts other fish with its bright colors. What benefit is there to the anemone?

INSIDE Information

Raccoons have long been held up as examples of "tidy" animals, dipping their food into water before they eat. But they are not washing it. Raccoons have small throats and cannot easily swallow large pieces of food. Rinsing food in water may help make it easier to swallow.

Most animals must work a little harder to get their food. Bees and butterflies, for example, must fly great distances to gather nectar from flowers. Birds, too, must fly a great deal to collect the insects, worms, and berries that they live on.

Many animals must hunt for food, often stalking prey for a long time over great distances. A leopard may travel several miles to bring down a jackal or an antelope. Most cats are hunters, as are many members of the dog family, great birds like the hawk and the eagle, and many kinds of snakes. These animals all pursue live prey, killing and eating their prey immediately or dragging it off to feed on for several days. Some snakes swallow their prey alive. After they consume a large meal, they do not have to hunt or eat again for days.

Still other animals set traps to get food. The trap-door spider, for example, digs a hole in the ground and builds a cover over it. Then it lurks just under the trap door, waiting for an insect to get close. When one does, the spider springs out and grabs it. Occasionally an insect will fall into the spider's hole and become trapped.

Many animals eat green plants. Moose, elk, rabbits, and springboks all eat low-shrub vegetation. Animals that eat plants are called *herbivores,* from *herba* (''vegetation'') and *vorare* (''to swallow up''). Animals that feed on other animals are called *carnivores.* What do you think *carn* means? It means ''flesh.'' Where does the word *carnal* come from? What does *voracious* mean? An *omnivore* eats both plants and animals. Where does the word *omnivore* come from?

Migration

When the food supply becomes low or scarce, animals have to travel to where there is more food. Sometimes this movement is unusual, caused by a drought or a fire, for instance. Sometimes such traveling is a regular event, a response to a seasonal change. Then it is called *migration.* Canada geese, salmon, arctic terns, whales, and even monarch butterflies migrate.

In October thousands of monarch butterflies migrate from the Canadian Rockies to Pacific Grove, California, 1,000 miles (1,609 km) away. Tortoises congregate in dens in the winters, move out in warmer weather, and return in the later fall.

Some aquatic animals, including fish, lobsters, crabs, prawns, and squids, migrate by moving from deep water in winter to the warmer surface for the summer. Lemmings, mouselike creatures in northern Europe, swarm in huge numbers about every five years, looking for new food sources. As they near the sea, many charge right into the water to their deaths. Destructive swarms of locusts eating every crop in sight are migrating from their breeding grounds because food has become scarce.

Large mammals such as caribou and reindeer migrate seasonally in search of food. Many birds nest in one type of climate and winter in another. They migrate along the same routes for both parts of their round trip. The chipping sparrow, red-winged blackbird, and many ducks nest in the northern part of the United States and into Canada and then move south to the Gulf of Mexico. The barn swallow and many warblers fly from their nests in Canada all the way to South or Central America. But the champion migrator is the arctic tern. It makes two round trips from the Arctic to the Antarctic every year, a total distance of nearly 22,000 miles. Fish can also be migratory animals. The common eel, found in streams and rivers in Europe, migrates more than 3,000 miles to breed. When the eels are mature, they make their way downstream and swim across the Atlantic Ocean to a warm, weedy area called the Sargasso Sea. The tiny young, newly hatched there, drift back towards Europe on strong sea currents.

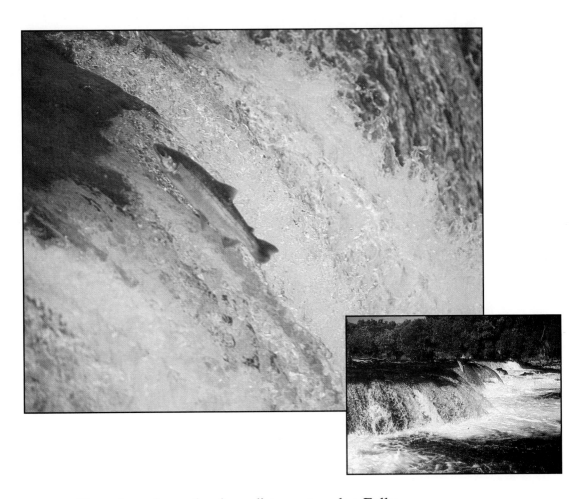

The salmon is another long-distance traveler. Fully grown salmon move from the sea towards the same gravel-bed streams where they were spawned. Sometimes as they fight their way upstream, they will leap over waterfalls 3 yards (3 m) high.

How do all of these animals find the best route? The question still puzzles scientists. They think perhaps some birds are able to navigate with the help of the position of the stars. Another theory is that birds use the magnetic field of the earth to guide them. Fish may sense chemicals in the water to direct them to their birthplace. How the creatures travel the same route every year is a mystery, but that they do it accurately is certain. Many birds even return to the same nest year after year.

Winter Preparations

"Go to the ant, thou sluggard; consider her ways, and be wise: Which having no guide, overseer, or ruler, provideth her meat in the summer, and gathereth her food in the harvest."

Proverbs 6:6-8

Other animals have different methods of coping with a changing food supply. Ants, the Bible says, store up food before winter. Squirrels, too, gather food during the summer, hoarding it for winter. They sometimes do not come back to the caches, however, and in the spring, new trees sprout from what was meant to be a winter's supper.

Skunks, brown bats, and hedgehogs have a different solution. They eat heartily during the summer, building up fat. Then they go to sleep for the winter. Some sleep through the entire season; others wake sluggishly periodically. Woodchucks, ground squirrels, and hamsters dig into deep burrows and sleep deeply all winter, their heart rate and breathing slowing way down. Why do you think their burrows must be deep? The lighter sleepers–like chipmunks and bears–sleep much of the time, but their breathing and heart rates stay near normal levels.

Some people think that the camel carries extra water in its hump. Actually, it has a store of fat in its hump or humps to use when food is scarce. But camels can go for days or even weeks without drinking water. Their woolly coats keep them from sweating away water too quickly.

Sometimes in the summer, reptiles and some amphibians are unable to get their normal food because the weather gets too dry and hot. In such cases they go into an inactive state until the weather changes. Alligators and turtles will dig themselves holes in the muddy bottoms of water holes or streams, climb in, cover the entrance with mud, and go to sleep. Since these animals have not built up a store of fat to live off, their bodies convert muscle into food.

There are different names for animals' inactive states. *Hibernation* comes from *hibernus* (''wintry''). *Estivation* comes from *aestivus* (''summery''). Which state do woodchucks go into? Which do reptiles go into?

Finding Out . . .

About Animal Behavior

1. Set up an aquarium or a hamster cage or plan to visit a zoo or a nature center. Or if you live on a farm or in the country, you may want to choose some animals you can observe easily.

2. Observe the animals for fifteen minutes three or four times during the day or, if possible, for several days. Write down everything you observe the animals doing. Perhaps you would like to read more about the animals you observe as well.

3. What can you conclude about the ways these animals communicate, get food, and give warnings? What do you notice about their daily routines? Write a report on all your observations.

Building Homes

Bears and other animals that hibernate or estivate usually do not build permanent homes. Bears, for example, choose a cave, a hollow tree, or–if unable to find anything better–a fallen tree to curl into or next to. They may choose a different spot every year. Caribou, elk, and most other deer simply bed down at night wherever they happen to be.

But some animals build permanent homes for themselves. Prairie dogs dig a network of tunnels and chambers, leaving them only if forced to. Some birds return year after year to the same nest or birdhouse, cleaning out and mending the old place for a new brood. Even spiders that weave webs intend to stay in that home until an accident destroys the web or the spider dies.

The beaver is an underwater engineer, constructing a sturdy lodge of branches and logs cemented with mud. The structure will have underwater entrance tunnels and feeding and living chambers above the water surface.

Wasps make paper houses and live communally like bees or ants. Their paper is made from finely chopped wood they have shredded and chewed, mixing it with saliva until its mass resembles papier-mâché. Wasps add layer upon layer until the house is complete. The layers may be multicolored depending on what kind of wood was gathered.

The red fox den has several entrances and tunnels up to 50 feet (15 m) long with chambers opening off them. Why do you think the den has so many entrances?

You think of birds when you hear the word *nest*, but the male Siamese fighting fish creates an underwater nest for his mate and her eggs. What do you think he uses? He uses bubbles mixed with a sticky mucus that strengthens the bubbles and holds them together.

The weaver birds in Africa construct a huge nest that houses 100 pairs of birds. The apartment houses might become as long as 16 feet (5 m) and are sometimes so heavy that they break the limbs of the trees to which they are attached.

Do you think building homes is an instinctive or a learned behavior? It is instinctive. The Baltimore oriole's nest is an elaborate structure, hanging like a deep pocket. Even an oriole that is hatched in a laboratory and that has never seen a nest is able to construct the typical oriole nest.

Often the need to protect and nurture young spurs an animal to build a home. Birds, for example, provide nests for their young. Animals that do not spend much time raising young have little need for a permanent–or even temporary–home. Sea turtles bury their eggs in the sand and then go back to the sea, never waiting until the eggs hatch.

And yet there are animals that take care of their young for long periods–even years–that never build homes. Elephants and whales both tend their young for several years, and both travel around constantly. Gorillas keep their young under their care for seven to ten years, never building anything more than a crude nest of branches for a night's sleep.

A Special Creation

God created man different from the animals. He gave man the great gift of language, the ability to learn from experience, the treasure of emotions. He also gave him the power to reason, to make decisions. This power is far beyond the simple moves an ape goes through in stacking boxes to get a banana above his reach. Man's power to reason is, indeed, at the center of his actions. We make choices, sometimes influenced by our emotions and sometimes by experience, but always we choose. Man does have a few reflexes and perhaps some instincts, but he is above all a thinking being. He has a spirit, a God-given soul, that will live forever. Thus man is responsible to use the intelligence he is given to make the right choices. Animals obey God's law by instinct. We have the privilege–and the responsibility–to obey God by free choice.

"Fear God, and keep his commandments: for this is the whole duty of man."

Ecclesiastes 12:13

 # The Biosphere

"But ask now the beasts, and they shall teach thee; and the fowls of the air, and they shall tell thee:

Or speak to the earth, and it shall teach thee: and the fishes of the sea shall declare unto thee.

Who knoweth not in all these that the hand of the Lord hath wrought this?"

Job 12:7-9

This is a meerkat. It is about 12 inches (30 cm) tall standing up, has a narrow nose, a stiff tail, long claws, and light gray fur, and is related to the mongoose. Now you know about the meerkat. Or do you?

Perhaps it would help if you understood that the meerkat's light fur helps him blend with his surroundings on the Kalahari Desert. He does not want to be seen by the falcons and the eagles overhead or the jackals and the foxes hunting nearby–all of which would like to eat him for lunch. His stiff tail helps him stand guard duty; he leans back on it like a brace. His long claws can be used for defense, but more often they dig up grubs and lizards from their hiding places in the sand.

Meerkats live in groups of up to thirty because life in the desert would be too hard and dangerous for one small meerkat on his own. He would have to watch the sky for enemies while he tried to dig for food. A large group, however, can divide the duties: some stand guard, some search for food, some tend the young, and some go out to fight if need be. One meerkat would be easy prey for the smallest fox; but ten meerkats, growling and hissing together in a mob, can scare off even a hungry jackal.

Now you know something about the meerkat. At least you understand him better. To study the entire world is impossible. To study white pines, porcupines, pineapples, stars, starfish, or yellow star-eyed grass is a little easier. Yet we can never really know about the particulars until we see how they fit into the whole. That whole is all the parts of the earth where life can exist, the *biosphere*. The name comes from *bios* ("life") and *sphaera* ("globe"). When you can see the whole picture, the specific details are no longer the end of learning; they are the beginning.

Not all living things can live in all parts of the biosphere. Have you ever seen a lizard on an iceberg? Do you think you would ever find a shark on the prairie? God has designed each animal to live in a certain place and has given it the best equipment for its needs.

The meerkat, for example, is well suited to the desert. Its long claws are essential for digging in the sand. Do you think it would be as able to get food in a swamp or a stream? How would its coat be a hindrance in a snowy region? All these questions show that it is difficult to study anything apart from its surroundings.

And it is difficult to decide just what an organism's surroundings truly are. If we want to study a salmon, for instance, we know we must consider the river as well. But should we also include the banks of the river? They do affect the water. And what about the forest or the fields beside the banks? A forest will influence the water in the river differently than a meadow will. Do you see the problem?

To help our study, we try to divide the biosphere into smaller areas. These divisions may be based on how much rain falls and what the temperature range is within a particular region.

Any such division, sometimes called an *ecosystem,* is made of living and nonliving parts. The physical part–the nonliving–includes water, sunlight, soil, and the physical structure of the land. Other physical influences might be fire and wind. If the division is mostly water, currents would be more important than wind, and fire would almost never be an influence. What other physical elements would be different in a water division?

The living part includes all the animal and plant populations in that certain area. How does the physical part determine the living part? Do you think the living part has any influence on the nonliving part?

All the organism populations in an area together make up a *community.* Wherever the animals live, whether in water, soil, air, or in or on some other living things, is called a *habitat.* What is a flea's habitat? What is an oxpecker's? What is the water buffalo's?

A large area may include several habitats and is the
sum of light, soil, air, and water there. *Habitat* comes
from *habitare* (''to dwell''). *Environment* comes from *en-*
(''in'') and *viron* (''circle''). How do these root meanings
help explain the difference between *habitat* and
environment? A habitat is where an animal lives precisely,
its ''address''–a bog, a sand dune, the forest floor, a group
of desert rocks. The animal's environment is the circle of
conditions around its habitat, the ''neighborhood.''

The broader term *ecosystem* means a section of the
earth including its soil, air, water, climate, minerals, and
all of the organisms that exist in it. The earth itself could
be called an ecosystem. But usually *ecosystem* refers to a
smaller area, such as a forest or a pond.

Divisions of the Biosphere

Major land divisions of the biosphere are called *biomes*. The last part of the name comes from *-ome* ("group"). What do you think the name means? A biome has somewhat defined boundaries and has a particular group of plants and animals. The temperatures, the soil, the rainfall, and the structure of the land will usually be nearly the same everywhere within a biome.

Tundra

Places where the earth is frozen ten months of the year, where the soil is thin and poor, where the ground never thaws more than 3 feet (1 m) down, may not at first seem likely to have any life in them. And even when the thaw comes, the melting snow and ice make most of the ground soggy. The ground that never thaws is called the *permafrost*. How does the permafrost cause bogs and shallow lakes to form? From what you know of erosion and soil, can you offer a theory to explain the poor soil of the region?

But even the sparse *tundra* is a biome. It supports lichens, mosses, grasses, and stunted trees that under other conditions would be towering evergreens. Among this hardy plant life, arctic foxes, musk oxen, ptarmigans, wolves, snowy owls, and hares live year round. During the summer thaw, other animals migrate into the tundra. Many kinds of birds nest there, and reindeer and caribou travel through. Insects hatch from millions of eggs laid the summer before. Why do you think so many birds come to the tundra to nest in the summer?

Coniferous Forest

Trees that bear cones are called *conifers;* forests that have mostly conifers in them are called *coniferous forests*. Can you name some trees that have cones? Spruces and firs grow in the northern parts of this biome. Pines and hemlocks grow in the southern parts. Which trees do you think grow better in slightly colder areas?

The tops of trees in a forest create a roof or *canopy*. The canopy of needles in a coniferous forest is so dense that little light falls to the forest floor. What do you think grows under the trees? Very few plants can grow in the dim light and in the kind of soil that needles form. Shrubs and grasses spring up at the forest edges.

This forest has two seasons, summer and winter, each about six months long. During the summer, the forest houses warblers and hawks as well as the year-round owls and woodpeckers and blue jays. Under the trees are moose, squirrels, rabbits, mice, elk, wolves, bears, and foxes. Where do you think the elk and deer mainly feed?

Deciduous Forest

The main trees in this biome are oaks, maples, elms, hickories, and yellow poplars. What do all these trees have in common? They all lose their leaves in the autumn. Trees that lose their leaves are *deciduous*. *Deciduous* comes from *decidere,* which means "to fall off." How do you think this forest floor is different from that of a coniferous forest? The soil is rich from the yearly fall and decay of leaves, and the canopy, which allows more light in, shelters much undergrowth. Ferns, mountain laurel, rhododendron, mosses, vines, and sumac abound. How do you think the undergrowth influences animal life?

Like the coniferous forest, this biome has bears, deer, and foxes. Many rabbits, mice, squirrels, and chipmunks dart about in the underbrush. In the trees are owls, hawks, and woodpeckers. There are also bobcats, skunks, raccoons, opossums, turkeys, thrushes, and sparrows in the deciduous forest. Why do you think there is a greater variety of animals here?

This biome has four distinct seasons, based on the cycle of the trees: autumn, when the leaves turn many colors and drop off; winter, when the limbs are bare and show no growth; spring, when the leaves begin to grow again; and summer, when the leaves grow and fill out the canopy once again. Do you think more people live near deciduous or coniferous forests? Why do you think so?

Grasslands

In places where small trees or bushes do not grow, a *grassland* flourishes. The short grasses that prosper attract such animals as prairie dogs, gophers, and other burrowing rodents. Why do you think that the grasslands also have many coyotes, wild dogs, and birds of prey? Grasslands are also home to zebras, antelope, and other grazing animals. In the United States the buffalo, or bison, once traveled in herds of more than a million across the open plains. What large carnivores do you think live on the grasslands?

Although some grasslands exist where there is plenty of rain, the dry summers keep trees from getting started. Fires break out on the dry grassland and spread fast, wiping out any seedlings that may have taken root. The grasses quickly return, as do the numerous insects that thrive there. Sometimes huge swarms of grasshoppers or locusts sweep over a grassland, eating every green thing in their path. This biome has many birds as well. Why do you think that is so? Prairie chickens and larks feed on the plentiful insect populations.

Grasslands are usually in the interiors of continents. They are well suited to farming. Why is that? What do you think is grown on the farms? Why do you think these regions are often called "breadbaskets"?

Desert

When you read the heading, perhaps you think of a hot, sandy wasteland where the sun beats down and nothing but a cactus or two can survive. But high temperatures do not cause a desert. Some deserts are cold, and some places with high temperatures are not deserts. The main condition that makes a place a desert is lack of rain. Less than 10 inches (25 cm) of rain a year in an area makes the ground and air dry.

The dryness causes other characteristics of the desert. Because the dry air cannot maintain even temperatures, the daytime temperatures in the desert are much higher than the nighttime temperatures. What kinds of animals and plants do you think are suited for living where there are wide differences in temperatures in one day?

INSIDE Information

Only a few places in the world are so dry that almost no life exists in them. We call them *absolute deserts.* The center of the Sahara Desert is one such place. Rain may come once every thirty or more years there. And when the rains do come, they fall over only small areas and end quickly.

Many desert animals are active at night. And God has given them special equipment to live in the desert. The meerkats are good examples. How are they fit for desert life? Desert foxes have large ears that help them get rid of body heat. What do you think the ears of arctic foxes are like? Tarantulas, reptiles such as Gila monsters, side-winders, and a few birds also have the necessary equipment to live full-time in this biome. Other birds and animals come in to hunt. Do you think most of the desert animals are large or small? Why do you think so?

Many of the plants are created to bloom only after periods of rain. Cacti grow in many deserts, for they can survive for long periods of time without water. Most desert plants have roots that do not go very deeply into the soil. But the roots go out from the plant in all directions for many yards. How does such a root system help the plants?

INSIDE Information

The kangaroo rats can live without drinking any water. They get enough water from the plants they eat. How does their staying underground during the day help them?

Tropical Rain Forests

Another biome that has warm days is the *tropical rain forest*. Unlike a desert, this forest gets 80 to 90 inches (200 to 225 cm) of rain per year. And although the nights are cooler than the days, the days are nearly the same all year long–hot and rainy. How do you think the vegetation is different from that in other biomes?

The canopy of a rain forest is made of the broad leaves of many kinds of trees. More than 150 kinds of trees can be found in a single rain forest. Why do you think this is so? Sometimes the canopy is so thick that nothing can grow on the forest floor. What other biome has a canopy that keeps many plants from growing underneath? If you were to visit a rain forest, you might feel that you were inside a big building with a very high ceiling. Some vines and wildflowers have their roots on the floor, but their stems wind up the trees, and their leaves and flowers are part of the canopy.

Where do you think most of the animals live in this biome? Monkeys, pythons, hummingbirds, toucans, and lizards live in the canopy, some never touching the ground their whole lives. Many varieties of insects also abound. There is plenty of food for all the animals. When do you think most of the animals are active?

Salt-Water Ecosystems

Almost three-fourths of the earth is covered by water. And almost all of that water is salt water. Although the *salt-water ecosystems* are vast, they are constant. The temperatures vary little in the oceans from day to day and season to season. Why do you think this is so?

Sunlight usually cannot reach more than 650 feet (200 m) into the sea. What does that fact tell you about the plants there? Where do you think you would find most of the life in the oceans? Why? The smallest plants in the ocean are *phytoplankton*. They are the food for the smallest animals, the *zooplankton*. Together these tiny plants and animals make up *plankton*, the main food for many other living things in the ocean, including the largest animal of all, the blue whale. The surface waters are an *open ocean* habitat.

Along the shores of oceans is another habitat, the place where the tides go in and out. Plants and animals that live here must have far different features from those in the open ocean. The starfish have tube feet something like suction cups that not only help them open clam shells but also help them hold to rocks in the wash of water and sand. The clams have shells that close tightly, and mussels and lobsters can dig themselves into the sand. Algae along the shores are designed to thrive both being underwater at high tide and being swept by waves at low.

Do you think there is a habitat at the ocean bottom? For years no one thought anything could exist in the darkness and the pressure on the ocean floor. Now we know that creatures such as the hatchetfish and the hammerfish live near warm springs in the deepest parts of the sea. Almost all the animals there are *bioluminescent;* that is, they produce their own light. Most of the animals have small eyes, large mouths, and stomachs that can stretch many times their normal size. Why do you think they have these features? What do you think they eat?

Freshwater Ecosystems

Any body of water that is not salty, such as a lake, swamp, pond, bog, river, spring, or stream, is a *freshwater ecosystem*. How would you classify these ecosystems into two groups? *Standing water* and *running water* have such different communities that most living things of one cannot live in the other.

Standing water habitats are not constant. Some are around only during certain times of the year. Can you think of such a standing water habitat in the tundra? The kinds of plants and animals in fresh water vary according to the depth and temperature of the water, the amount of sunlight, the amount of oxygen and minerals in the water, and the rates at which water comes and goes. Do you think there is more oxygen in swift water or still water? Where do you think the most active fish live?

The populations in fresh water fit into one of four groups: those that live on the bottom of the habitat, those that float on the water or in the current, those that move about in the water, and those that live some part of their lives in the water and some part near it. How would you classify a salmon? What about a turtle?

A cypress swamp is the natural home for the alligator.
It swims in the shallow water and suns on the roots of the
cypress trees. Otters, foxes, raccoons, herons, egrets, and
storks all use the protruding cypress roots for landing
places where they can survey the area for food. The
cypress trees are sometimes 100 feet (30 m) tall and perhaps 600 years old. Do you think there is a different
community in the top of a cypress tree?

In a cypress swamp, Everglades minks hunt for fish.
Plants rooted at the bottom of the swamp spread their
leaves over the surface. What land biome has plants that
produce leaves and flowers high above their roots to get
the sun? Other plants live under the water. Frogs,
salamanders, and many kinds of snakes flourish, feeding
on the insects. Worms and snails rest on the bottom of the
swamp. What else do you think the snakes eat? Why are
there no rabbits in this habitat?

216

Interaction in the Biosphere

Every population in an area affects the other populations, either directly or indirectly. We try to describe this *interaction* by making diagrams that show what animals eat. Plants, because they do not eat but are eaten, are called *producers.* Animals that eat only plants are called *primary consumers.* The name means "first eater." Animals that eat the plant-eaters are called *secondary consumers.* In what way are they "second eaters"? Bacteria that break down the remains of dead plants and animals are *decomposers.* Their activity returns nutrients to the soil. How are they important to the whole ecosystem?

Can you name the producers and consumers in this picture? Which do you think is primary, and which is secondary? Select one member of the community to be removed. What do you think would be the effect on the rest of the community?

The Food Chain

The simplest description of the interaction of producers and consumers is the *food chain*. Why do you think it is called a "chain"?

The energy that all living things need comes from the sun. How do herbivores get most of their energy from the sun? How do carnivores? Why is it important that all the links in the chain be present? What might happen if a drought dried up all the grass? What would happen if all the hawks died? What would happen if a disease wiped out the rabbit population? Could the grass continue to grow if decomposers died out?

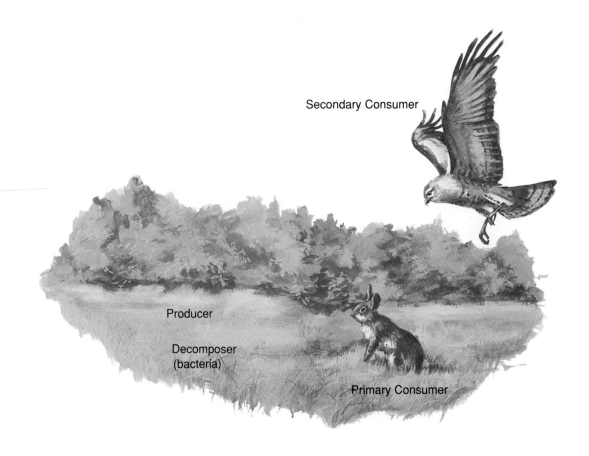

Secondary Consumer

Producer

Decomposer
(bacteria)

Primary Consumer

The Food Web

Why is a food chain not a complete picture of the interaction of an ecosystem? Not all animals eat only one kind of animal or plant. To show the overlapping of food chains, we use a *food web*.

Why do animals like rabbits and mice produce many young often? What would happen if all the wolves left the area? What would cause wolves to leave? How would a plague of grasshoppers change this web?

The Food Pyramid

As you saw in the food web, some animals are eaten in greater numbers than others, and some animals are not eaten at all. Which population in the food web do you think uses more of the available energy in a place–rabbit or hawk? The rabbits do. To show how much energy different members of a food web use, we make a *food pyramid*.

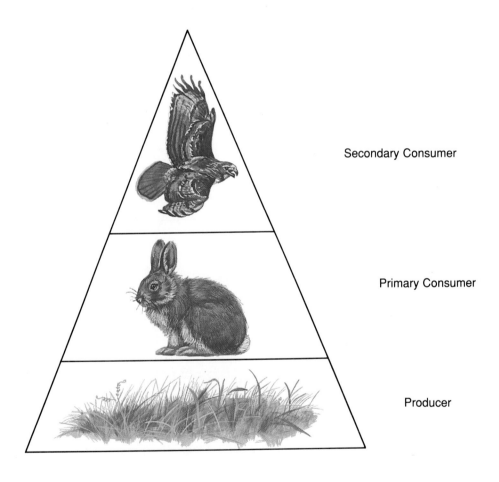

Secondary Consumer

Primary Consumer

Producer

Why are the plants on the bottom of the pyramid? Why are the secondary consumers at the top? Why do the levels get smaller as they go up?

Time Rhythms in the Biosphere

In the Kalahari Desert, the sun is going down. The meerkats return to their dens after a day of foraging for food among the blackthorns and the sparse grasses. They lick each other and settle down together. In a little while, they all sleep. At first light the next day, they will wake and set forth again, clawing after scorpions, guarding the young, and standing sentinel. They live day by day the same way, in a cycle of eating and sleeping and watching.

As the meerkats go into their dens, other animals begin to wake from their day's sleep and come out to hunt for food. The animals' actions form a repeating pattern we call a *rhythm*. The changeover that occurs when some animals go to sleep and other ones stir is part of the *daily rhythm* in an environment. The rhythm includes the eating and resting cycles of all the animals in an area.

The change from winter to spring to summer to fall causes a *seasonal rhythm*. What effect does the change of season have on animals that migrate? Animals that do not migrate respond to the seasonal rhythm in other ways. The arctic hare, for example, has brown fur during the summer. As winter nears, his fur turns white to match the snow. Can you think of other ways animals respond to the seasons?

God has made each animal and plant to suit its environment, equipping it to survive and reproduce, providing it with a "clock," and giving it a part to fill in the orderly design of the biosphere.

Finding Out . . .

About Interaction

1. Get a 20-gallon glass tank with a glass cover, enough fine gravel to cover the bottom of the tank, a pound of perlite, 3 pounds of activated charcoal, a pound of sphagnum moss, a plastic margarine container, two snails, a tree frog, a small bag of peat moss, a small fern plant, a violet plant, some live crickets, some distilled water, and perhaps a pitcher plant. (Garden centers and nurseries will probably have the perlite and the plants. Plants that can take much moisture can be substituted. Pet stores may have snails and tree frogs.)

2. Spread perlite evenly on the bottom of the tank, and then put the gravel layer in. Next, put in a half-inch layer of charcoal. Put down a half-inch layer of peat moss, and pack it firmly. Add the rest of the peat moss without packing it. Make a slope up to one side. In the lowest area, put the margarine container filled with water.

3. Place the plants in the peat moss, putting the pitcher plant (if you have one) in the low area. Give the plants enough room to grow. Put sphagnum moss over the whole surface, and water it lightly. Place the snails, the crickets, and the frog in the tank, and put the glass cover on. Put the tank where it will get only indirect light and where it will have day and night.

4. Observe the "bog" every day. Make a diagram of any interaction you see. Where might such a habitat occur in nature? Once you see a food web established, remove one member of the community. Record what happens.

About Communities in a Habitat

1. Get a notebook and a pencil. You may also want to take a camera. Find a small habitat, such as a fallen log, the bank of a pond or lake, or a section of a field or undeveloped lot.

2. Observe the habitat without disturbing it. If you observe on a bank or in a field or lot, mark off an area about 2 feet by 2 feet with string or rulers. List the plants and animals that you see there. What may be part of the community that you do not see? What animals come and go? Which ones live in the habitat? Can you predict any ways the area will change if it receives heavy rains? If there is no rain for several days?

3. Go back to the habitat in a week or two. List what you see this time. What changes have there been? What do you think caused the changes? Write a report on your observations. Use diagrams to illustrate.

Finding Out . . .

About Water Ecosystems

1. Get two large glass jars with lids, some distilled water, some salt water, some sand, some living pond plants, and two pieces of cardboard the size of the jar bottoms. (If you live near a pond or lake, you can get plants there. If not, you can buy suitable plants from a pet store.)

2. Put an inch of sand in the bottom of each jar. Put the same number and kinds of plants in each jar, being sure the roots are firmly set in the sand. Put a piece of cardboard on top of the sand to hold it in place as you add water. Then slowly fill one jar with salt water and the other with distilled water. Take the cardboard out, and put on the lids.

3. Set both jars in an area where they will get indirect light and a night-and-day cycle. Observe the jars every day for a week. Which plants do better?

 # Balance of Nature

"O Lord, how manifold are thy works! in wisdom hast thou made them all: the earth is full of thy riches."

Psalm 104:24

When God called the earth out of nothing, He hung it on nothing, just far enough from the sun to keep life from burning or freezing. He started the earth spinning and sent it traveling around the sun. On the earth, the days and nights began their orderly succession. Then the seasons began to come in turns, resting and renewing the earth continually.

On the mountains, in the seas, under the soil, on the plains, in the deserts and forests, plants and animals live in the flux of the seasons, under the coming and going of day and night. Every plant and animal is perfectly designed for its environment, each serving a purpose in the great design of our world.

Man has always been awed by the complex interaction of plants, animals, earth, water, and air. His study of how all these parts affect each other is called *ecology. Oikos* ("house") becomes *eco-*. What house do you think might be meant here?

226

When many people hear the word *ecology,* they think of oil spills, holes in the ozone, and endangered species lists. Lately these topics have been the main interest of many people, but to study them and nothing else gives a warped view of ecology. To truly learn about the biosphere, we must have a bigger perspective. We must view as much as we can of the whole "house."

Design in the Earth

You know already that there are rhythms in the biosphere, repetitions of light and dark, warmth and cooling. There are other patterns as well that encompass those rhythms, that depend all at one time on earth and air and water.

Water circulates in the biosphere constantly. It evaporates from ponds and oceans, from plants and animals. It falls again as rain and snow, settling into the soil, filtering into the water under the ground, running into rivers and swamps. Water makes life possible here; its presence is one important difference between Earth and the other planets.

When the water falls, it adds nitrogen to the soil. It also weathers rocks and breaks up hard ground, making more soil. Rivers and streams and floods carry soil from one place to another, sometimes even into the seas. The oceans receive much of the water that runs off the land, but the rivers are never emptied, and the sea never overflows. God has set the cycle for the water, and only He can overrule it, as when He sent the Flood.

The rocks that become soil under the beating rains come from the earth. Some are belched out of volcanoes, some are carved out of sediment by blowing sand and frost and pressure, and some are exposed by the wearing wind and passing time. Eventually rocks become soil, under the sun and in the cold, swept by wind and water, penetrated by the roots of plants.

The plants draw nutrients from the soil, but when the grass withers and the trees in old age fall and decay, the nutrients go again into the ground. They have been *recycled*. The water and the minerals have been only borrowed after all. Long before man thought about things being biodegradable, God had established natural processes for decomposition.

Finding Out . . .

About Water Cycles

1. Get the "bog" from *Finding Out About Interaction,* or get a large glass jar with a lid, some potting soil, some sand, some water, and a small living plant.

2. If you are using the glass jar, put a layer of sand in the bottom and then a layer of soil. Place the plant firmly in the soil, and water it carefully, being careful not to make the soil muddy. Put the lid on the jar, and set the terrarium where it will get sunlight.

3. Observe the bog or the terrarium. What do you think will happen when the sun warms the interior? Why does it happen? How does the bog or terrarium benefit? What would happen if the water supply were reduced? Can you think of a way to reduce the water supply and see what happens? What are some ways the balance can be restored?

Finding Out . . .

About Natural Recycling

1. Get 100 toothpicks, a balance scale, a paring knife, a cucumber or a potato, and any other fruits or vegetables you want to try.

2. Peel the cucumber or the potato, and cut it into tiny pieces. Put the toothpicks on one side of the scale. Then add pieces of the cucumber or potato on the other side of the scale until the scale balances. Set the scale in a warm or sunny place.

3. Later check the scale. Has it become unbalanced? Remove toothpicks one at a time until the scale balances again. Count the toothpicks you have taken off. What percentage of the vegetable was water? What happened to the water?

4. Try other kinds of fruits and vegetables. You might try putting a small amount of chopped potato in the ''bog'' you made for *Finding Out About Interaction*. Compare the rate of evaporation there with the rate outside the tank. What does the potato return to the ecosystem besides water?

About Biodegradable Material

1. Get a candy wrapper, a freshly picked leaf, some water, a few small stones, and a little loose soil.

2. Find a place outside to lay the candy wrapper and the leaf. Try to find a place that will be away from walkways and will not likely be disturbed. Spread the loose soil in about one square foot. Lightly sprinkle the soil with water. Place the open candy wrapper and the leaf on the soil. Put some small stones on them to hold them down.

3. Leave the wrapper and the leaf untouched for several days, but observe both daily and record the changes in each. What difference does rain make on both? How does the sun change the objects? Is the wrapper biodegradable?

While plants live, they take carbon dioxide from the air and put oxygen and carbon dioxide into it. Man and animals breathe in the air, using the oxygen and breathing out carbon dioxide. The atmosphere is constantly in the process of exchange and yet constantly the same.

The rain that falls also depends on the air. Without the heating and cooling of air and the colliding of masses of air, there would be no rain. Without the thin band of air around our earth to hold in the day's warmth, we would freeze at night. And during the day, ultraviolet rays would scorch us. Yet the sun filters through that shimmering veil and powers everything that lives on the earth.

INSIDE Information

Only about twenty-one per cent of our atmosphere is oxygen. Perhaps you wonder why God did not make it easier for us to breathe by making the percentage greater. God in His providence has carefully balanced the composition of the air with the needs of all His living things. We have enough oxygen to breathe. Any more in the air might cause fires to burn out of control and might upset the balance for plants.

The Continuous Balance

Within the great cycles of water and soil and air, the food webs, the migrations, the births, and the deaths continue. The caribou migrate. The wolves follow them, bringing down the weak, the old, the slow. A herd, stronger in the end for the losses, grazes on lichens and grasses in the tundra. If the wolves did not hunt, what might eventually happen?

The wolves eat what they can of the caribou carcass. Then the scavenger birds clean the bones. The bones are gnawed by small animals such as mice. The last remains are reduced by bacteria and finally become part of the soil. From the soil springs the reindeer moss, which is eaten by another generation of caribou.

And so it goes in every ecosystem, the constant decline and growth, the decaying and the sprouting. God has designed all parts of the biosphere to function best in balance, and He has provided means by which things stay in balance. The caribou herd, kept in check by the wolves, does not overgraze the plants and face starvation. The wolves, able to kill and eat only so many caribou, do not become too numerous and wipe out the caribou. In a balanced ecosystem, all the populations stay about the same size.

Man cannot reasonably study the composition of air, the interconnectedness of all living things, the precision of the turning of the earth, or the splendor of a single lily without seeing the hand of our wise and good God.

Yet not all men are reasonable. To acknowledge a Creator is to admit responsibility to Him. Rather than serve the God who made all things, some men choose to say there is no God and to find other ways to explain the order and consistency they see in their gardens and through their telescopes.

People who think that it is foolish to believe the account of Creation put their faith in false theories. It seems more reasonable to them that the universe resulted from a lucky combination of gases, that life on the earth, in all its infinite variety and harmony, developed from one cell, that chanced to get exactly the perfect conditions. They must believe that by incredible chance the planets travel at exactly the right speeds to stay in their orbits, and that their orbits just happen to allow for the safest flow of traffic possible. They believe it is just another accident that all the billions and billions of galaxies we know of operate on the same principles. Such theories lead man not only away from God but also into every other kind of illogic.

Man's Role

God commanded Adam to subdue the earth and to have dominion over the animals (Gen. 1:28). Noah was told to kill animals for food. The earth and what is in it are for man's use. But the Lord also instructed Adam to tend the garden of Eden, "to dress it and to keep it." And He told Noah to take animals with him into the ark, "to keep seed alive upon the face of all the earth" (Gen. 7:3). Man's responsibility is clearly part of his privilege.

When man tames an animal, he becomes responsible for its life. He must give it food, water, shelter, rest, and attention. When he plows and plants a field, man must take care that the way he plows and what he plants are not wasteful of the soil. When he mines the treasures from the ground, he is to get only what he needs.

Man's dominion is not an exclusive right to squander. It is a commandment to be a careful steward of things that are not his. Some people, believing that there is no God and that man is wholly in charge of life on the earth, say that we should not touch anything in nature. They begin to believe that man is an intruder, a blight on nature. How did they arrive at such an idea?

When man does not accept God as Master, he puts himself in service to something else. Many times since the world began, men have turned to nature as a god. In our time, many are worshipping the planet as a god. They are devout worshippers, dedicating a day to the celebration of their god and avenging themselves on others who they think are opposing their religion.

Like all false religions, theirs is built on fear, fear that our resources will run out, that the sun will blaze through an ozone weakened by pollution, that all the water will be poisoned, that the earth will be broiled by the *greenhouse effect*. The evidence they present seems plausible, and many are persuaded by it to join the worship of Earth.

What should be the Christian's response to all of this? First, he must be confident that the God who made the world is able to maintain it. Then he must see that he lives a proper life, a life directed by God's Word. If a Christian is unselfish, careful, compassionate, just, faithful, and humble as he ought to be, he will never be guilty of abusing the natural world.

We need to take our role as manager of the earth seriously. Are we careful with the things directly in our charge? Do we leave lights on for no reason? Do we throw away food because we cooked too much? Are we kind and caring masters of our tame animals? And do we think about how our actions will affect our testimony to people caught in the dread of the death of the planet?

Furthermore, we should learn as much as we can of true science so that we can evaluate statements about the biosphere. What about the hole in the ozone? Have the reports considered the replacement of ozone with every lightning bolt that flares in the sky? What about global warming? Have the reports on that been based on records–records of observations–from just a few years? Can we say for sure that the recent warming is a dangerous sign and not rather part of a much bigger cycle?

The study of science–that is, the observation and description of God's creation–will keep us from accepting ideas based on guesses and on evidence poorly collected or presented. It will remind us of the great gift the earth is and of our duties in it. It will also keep us mindful of how great a God we serve.

Veterinary Science

A *veterinarian* is a doctor for animals. Veterinarians work primarily with tame animals, although they may be called on from time to time to set broken wings of wild birds or to give attention to ailing bears or injured raccoons.

Vets give medicine to and do surgery on sick animals. But they also instruct owners about the proper diets and care for their pets. It is better to keep your cocker spaniel's ears clean than to have it treated for mites later. By taking blood samples and keeping records such as weight gain or loss, a vet can detect a problem early and prevent an animal from becoming seriously ill.

Besides studying animal anatomy, chemistry, and medicine, a vet needs a good knowledge of animal behavior. Why do you think this is so?

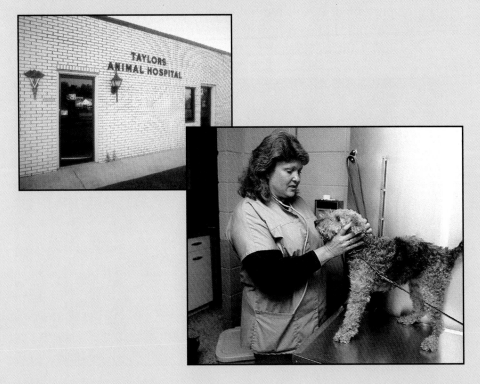

Science in ACTION

Wildlife Management

A *wildlife management specialist* works in national parks and in wildlife preserves, special lands set aside for wild animals. In some parks, like Yellowstone, specialists keep records of elk and deer populations, recording causes for increases and decreases. They also take note of the animals' responses to influences such as weather and man. What sciences do the specialists use in their work?

Not all national parks are forests. Part of Lake Malawi in southeast Africa is the world's first freshwater national park. Most of the park is underwater. What special skills do you think the management specialists need there? The park was established to protect and study species of fish that are found nowhere else.

Wildlife specialists sometimes work with *animal geneticists*. These scientists study how animals are alike or different from their parents. When do you think geneticists are especially useful in wildlife management? If the specialists are studying animals that are rare, geneticists may be able to find ways to help increase the animals' population. Geneticists also study inherited diseases. How would that study help specialists?

The Puritan preacher Jonathan Edwards tells that he killed a bird when he was young merely for the sport of killing. Then he discovered the nest of baby birds calling for food. Unable to care for them and not wanting them to starve, he had to kill them also. Then, he says, he understood that "even the tender mercies of the wicked are cruel."

To be a wise master, man must learn all he can about his world, and he must understand God's principles set forth in the Bible and act on them consistently. Man is allowed mastery, but not tyranny. He is to use the earth's living and nonliving resources for his needs, thinking ahead, managing well what is put in his charge.

Plants and animals are indispensable to man. They provide him food, clothing, beauty, balance, and insight. And they can warn man when he has overstepped his rule and threatens to hurt even himself with unwise dominion. Only by learning to use the earth as God intended–wisely, justly, humbly, remembering who is Creator and who is only caretaker–can man truly fulfill his responsibility to "replenish the earth, and subdue it." For though he is master, man should remember that there is much he can learn from his charge.

"Thou art worthy, O Lord, to receive glory and honour and power: for thou hast created all things, and for thy pleasure they are and were created."

Revelation 4:11

Glossary

absolute magnitude a measure of how bright a star actually shines

adaptation an adjustment to conditions within hereditary limits

air resistance friction caused by an object passing through the atmosphere

alchemist *(al′kə•mist)* one who believes elements can be turned into other elements

allergy a condition caused by hypersensitive response to materials in the air

animal population animals of the same kind living together

antitoxin *(an′tē•tok′sin)* a substance that makes a toxin harmless

Apollo 11 the first manned spacecraft to land on the moon

apparent magnitude a measure of how bright a star appears from Earth

artery *(är′tər•ē)* a vessel carrying blood away from the heart

asthma *(az′mə)* a disorder that causes the small tubes in the lungs to become narrow

astronaut one who travels in space

astronautics a study of what traveling in space requires

astronomer a scientist who studies outer space

Big Bang an evolutionary theory of how the universe began

binary stars *(bī′nə•rē)* stars that revolve around each other

bioluminescence *(bī′ō•loo′mə•nes′əns)* the ability of some animals to produce their own light

biome *(bī′ōm)* a major land division of the biosphere

biosphere *(bī′ə•sfîr′)* the sum of all the parts of the earth where life can exist

black hole an intense field of gravity produced by the collapse of a massive star

caldera *(kal•dâr′ə)* a basin at the top of a volcano

canopy the roof formed by the tops of trees in a forest

cardiologist *(kär′dē•ol′ə•jist)* one who studies the heart

cardiology *(kär′dē•ol′ə•jē)* the study of the heart

carnivore *(kär′nə•vôr)* a meat eater

chemical symbol the letter or letters representing the name of an element

chemistry the study of the different kinds of matter

cilia *(sil′ē•ə)* hairlike structures capable of rhythmical motion

community all the organism populations in an area

compound a combination of two or more different elements involving a chemical change

constellation a pattern that stars are imagined to form

decomposer an organism that breaks down dead plant and animal material

diaphragm *(dī′ə•fram′)* a strong sheet of muscle attached to the lower ribs and the backbone

echolocation *(ek′ō•lō•kā′shən)* the means of orienting by reflected sound waves used by animals such as the bat

ecosystem *(ek′ō•sis•təm)* a division of the biosphere often based on rainfall and temperature range within a region

element matter made of only one kind of atom

environment the sum of light, soil, air, and water in an area

epicenter the point on the earth's surface directly above the focus of an earthquake

epiglottis *(ep′i•glot′is)* a thin flap of tissue that can close off the trachea

esophagus *(i•sof′ə•gəs)* the foodpipe

estivation *(es′tə•vā′shən)* a state of inactivity during hot, dry weather

fault the line along which crustal plates touch

fission *(fish′ən)* the splitting apart of atoms

focus the point along which crustal plates slip

food chain the simplest description of the interaction of producers and consumers

food pyramid a description of energy consumption in an ecosystem

food web a description showing the overlapping of food chains

formula *(fôr′myə•lə)* an equation that represents a chemical reaction

friction a rubbing force between two objects

fusion *(fyōō′zhən)* the combination of nuclei

galaxy *(gal′ək•sē)* a collection of stars

Geiger counter *(gī′gər)* a machine that counts the number of rays or particles that strike its sensor

geyser *(gī′zər)* a hot spring with fountain action

gravity the pull of one body on another

habitat *(hab′ə•tat)* a specific place where an animal lives

hay fever a common allergy

heart the pump of the circulatory system

heart rate the number of times the heart beats in a given period

herbivore *(hûr′bə•vôr′)* a plant eater

hibernation *(hī′bər•nā′shən)* a state of inactivity during winter

host-parasite relationship an association between two organisms that may be harmful to one

imaging a technique by which photographs are sent from outer space to Earth

inertia *(in•ûr′shə)* the resistance to a change in position

instinct *(in′stingkt′)* the behavior animals are born knowing

isotope *(ī′sə•tōp′)* one of two or more atoms with the same number of protons but different numbers of neutrons

larynx *(lar′ingks)* the voice box

lava *(lä′və)* magma that spills onto the earth's surface

law a statement that is made after many observations of the same occurrence

learned behavior an action resulting from trial and error

lungs fleshy bags where oxygen enters the blood stream

magma *(mag′mə)* liquid rock

magnitude a number representing the size of seismic waves

marrow tissue in the center of the bone

matter all material in the universe; anything that takes up space and has weight

micrometeoroid *(mī′krō•mē′tē•ə•roid′)* a tiny meteor

migration *(mī•grā′shən)* regular travel as a response to a seasonal change

mixture a combination of two or more substances involving only a physical change

motion the process of changing position

mucus *(myōō′kəs)* a thick, sticky substance in the respiratory tract

nebula *(neb′yə•lə)* a cloud of gas and dust between stars

Newton's first law the observation that objects in motion tend to stay in motion

Newton's second law the observation that it is easier to change the position of a light object than a heavy one

Newton's third law the observation that every action has an equal and an opposite reaction

nova *(nō′və)* a variable star that suddenly increases in brightness to several times its normal magnitude

nuclear medicine the branch of medicine that uses different kinds of radiation to detect or treat disease

nucleus *(nōō′klē•əs)* the center of an atom

obsidian *(ob•sid′ē•ən)* a glassy igneous rock

omnivore *(om′nə•vôr′)* a plant and meat eater

oxidizer *(ok′sə•dī′zər)* a device that supplies oxygen to burn fuel

parallax *(par′ə•laks′)* a change in position that provides a new line of sight

parasite *(par′ə•sīt′)* an organism that benefits from another without providing benefit in return

permafrost *(pûr′mə•frôst′)* ground in the tundra that never thaws

plankton *(plangk′tən)* tiny plants and animals in the ocean

plasma *(plaz'mə)* a yellow liquid in the blood

plate in theory, one of the large moving sections of the earth's crust

platelet a cell fragment that starts the clotting process in blood

primary consumer a member of an ecosystem that feeds on producers

probe an unmanned spaceship or satellite that has scientific equipment

producer a member of an ecosystem at the bottom of the food chain

propellant *(prə•pel'ənt)* a fuel that provides the thrust for an engine

pulsar *(pul'sär')* another name for a radio star

pulse the little jump in the blood vessels with every heart-beat

pumice *(pum'is)* a porous igneous rock

radioactivity *(rā'dē•ō•ak'tiv'ə•tē)* the process of giving off particles and energy from the nucleus

red cell a cell in the blood that carries oxygen

reflex an inborn response to stimulus

respiration an exchange of gases; breathing

rhyolite *(rī'ə•līt')* a fine-grained igneous rock

rhythm a repeating pattern

ring of fire a band along which many earthquakes and volcanoes occur

secondary consumer a member of an ecosystem that feeds on primary consumers

seismic waves *(sīz'mik)* vibrations in the earth during an earthquake

seismograph *(sīz'mə•graf')* a machine which records earthquake vibrations

seismology *(sīz•mol'ə•jē)* the study of earthquakes

simulator *(sim'yə•lā'tər)* an apparatus that generates test conditions nearly like actual conditions, such as the specially built, computer-controlled room that provides space conditions on the earth

solar system a star and a group of planets

sphygmomanometer *(sfig′mō•mə•nom′i•tər)* a special machine for measuring blood pressure

Sputnik *(sput′nik)* the world's first artificial satellite

star cluster many stars that appear bound together

stethoscope *(steth′ə•skōp′)* a device for listening to sounds within the body

symbiosis *(sim′bē•ō′sis)* the relationship of two or more different organisms that may be helpful to each

thrust the force that pushes a rocket forward

toxin *(tok′sin)* a poison

trachea *(trā′kē•ə)* the windpipe

traction friction that stops unwanted motion

trajectory *(trə•jek′tə•rē)* the path of a moving body

transfusion *(trans•fyoo′zhən)* the process of transferring blood

tremor *(trem′ər)* a mild earthquake

tsunami *(tsoo•nä′mē)* a massive tidal wave

valve a small gate in the heart

variable star a star that fluctuates in brightness

vein a vessel carrying blood toward the heart

vent a crack or hole in the upper mantle and crust

white cell a cell that protects the body against infection

zodiac *(zō′dē•ak′)* a chart that represents the path of the sun, moon, planets, and stars across the sky

Index

Photo Credits